ROBERT A.M. STERN ARCHITECTS

BUILDINGS AND PROJECTS
2010–2014

To
Clive Aslet
with best wishes,

Robert Stern

ROBERT A.M. STERN ARCHITECTS

BUILDINGS AND PROJECTS
2010–2014

Edited by Peter Morris Dixon and Jonathan Grzywacz

THE MONACELLI PRESS

Preface

The past is an inexhaustible storehouse of apt attitudes and adaptable ideals; it opens of itself at the touch of desire; it yields up, now this treasure, now that, to anyone who comes to it armed with a capacity for personal choices.[1]

—Van Wyck Brooks

With this volume, it is a privilege to document five years of extraordinary growth and diversification in which my partners and I welcomed not only an increasing range of building types, but also growth in our global reach, bringing new challenges and new perspectives. We pride ourselves on being nimble and eager to take on all kinds of projects. Yet as we have grown we have endeavored to stay true to our principles, taking each commission on its own terms, bringing to it all we have learned and seeking to develop new knowledge through close observation. Our search continues for an architecture that succeeds by virtue of its ability to connect; to be inventive yet somehow familiar; to be present but not obtrusive; to be the setting, and not the performance, in the drama of daily life.

When I set out on this path more than forty years ago, I began with a search for a distinctly American architecture, as one possible alternative to the bland placelessness of International Style modernism. In that search I was inspired by Van Wyck Brooks's 1918 essay "On Creating a Usable Past," which I had studied in college. Brooks's essay presented the idea that as we look to history we ask, "What out of all the multifarious achievements and impulses and desires of the American . . . mind, ought we to elect to remember?" New research in the history and theory of American architecture such as my professor Vincent Scully's *The Shingle Style* (1955) helped guide my initial search. Robert Venturi's *Complexity and Contradiction in Architecture* (1966) then encouraged me to look beyond America, and also beyond the established canon of European modernism, to explore the lessons of underappreciated masters and undervalued vernaculars across a wide span of time and place in order to help find architectural expression for today and tomorrow.

In the past five years we have been privileged to expand our international presence to include India and China, working with clients who have traveled internationally and returned home with high expectations for a future that includes a deepening respect for local architectural traditions, which have been regrettably neglected and in many cases obliterated in the past half-century. It has not been our approach to impose on our international work a predetermined point of view, whether an American style, or a quixotic universal language. Engaging with cultures that are new to us enables us to once again embark on a journey toward the discovery of a usable past and to look for ways to fulfill the desires of a cosmopolitan society longing to reconnect with its own history and with other cultures. These discoveries have inspired us and refreshed us. It has been, in a sense, a rediscovery of first principles; journeys abroad that have led us homeward.

As our practice has matured, the scale of the enterprise has grown with it, so that now we are sixteen design partners, some of whom have been part of our leadership for a very long time. The partners benefit from an intelligent, energetic cadre of inquiring young minds attracted to our firm by our way of doing things. This is an affirmation that our approach continues to resonate even as the digital revolution leads some architects down strange highways of abstraction and self-reference. Our mixture of experienced hands with new talents bodes very well for the future, and I thank one and all for their creative input and professionalism.

An architect is only as good as his clients. We are also indebted to innumerable professional collaborators from related fields who enrich our work; without them we would be lost. I also thank those who have worked with me to document our progress over the last five years in this book, in particular our editors, Peter Morris Dixon and Jonathan Grzywacz, who with Shannon Hohlbein, Monica Gaura, Charmee Donga, and John Gibson organized the material that tells our story in words and images. We continue to enjoy a longstanding collaboration with Pentagram, and we acknowledge the design team for this book: Michael Bierut, Yve Ludwig, and Laitsz Ho. We are grateful both to the many artists who help us represent our buildings before construction and to the photographers who capture our completed buildings for the page, with special thanks to Peter Aaron, who has been documenting our work almost from the start, and his protégé Francis Dzikowski. And as ever, I thank our publisher, Gianfranco Monacelli, for giving us the opportunity to share our work with audiences old and new, and his managing editor Elizabeth White and senior editor Alan Rapp, who have guided us through the publication process.

—Robert A.M. Stern

1. Van Wyck Brooks, "On Creating a Usable Past," *The Dial*, April 11, 1918, 337-41.

Contents

Buildings and Projects
2010–2014

The Clarendon / One Back Bay

Boston, Massachusetts
2003–2010
Project Partners:
Paul L. Whalen
Michael D. Jones

Right: View from John
Hancock Tower plaza.

Amidst a complex urban setting where Back Bay meets the South End, the Clarendon, a 32-story residential tower, dynamically aggregates 60-foot cubes to suggest traditional masonry blocks stepping up to form an iconic point tower that holds its own next to the taller reflective John Hancock Tower (I.M. Pei & Partners, 1976) diagonally across the street. A five-story limestone base enlivens the streetscape with shopfronts and separate entrances to the rental and the condominium residences. Above, the building sets back to create communal rooftop terraces.

The design satisfies a municipal mandate for contemporary expression even as its palette of red brick and limestone is typical for residential architecture in the Back Bay. Brick facades are boldly expressed as curtain-wall—no pretense here that they are load-bearing—and the glass slots that demarcate the cubes reinforce the impression of lightness.

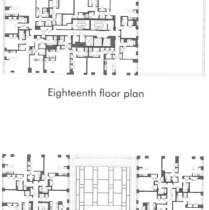

Eighteenth floor plan

Third floor plan

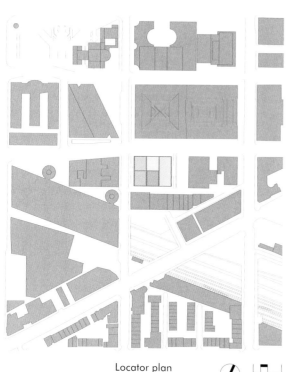

Locator plan

0 75 150 ft

Ground floor plan

0 16 32ft

Left: View across
Back Bay.

Right top: View
looking west along
Stuart Street.

Right bottom: Crown
at dusk.

Left: Entry at the Clarendon.

Right top: Clarendon lobby.

Right middle: Clarendon library.

Right bottom: One Back Bay lobby.

Arthur and Janet Ross Children's Addition

East Hampton Library
East Hampton, New York
2001–2014
Project Partner:
Randy M. Correll

Carrying forward the character of the Library's original building (1910) by Aymar Embury II, together with our 1997 addition, the Ross wing incorporates a children's reading room, an art gallery, and an auditorium suitable for public lectures and film screenings. The same vocabulary as the original building—stucco and half-timbering above brick wainscoting—ensures that it all looks of a piece. The playful fit-out of the children's room by Lee H. Skolnick fully respects the paneling and open truss-work we developed.

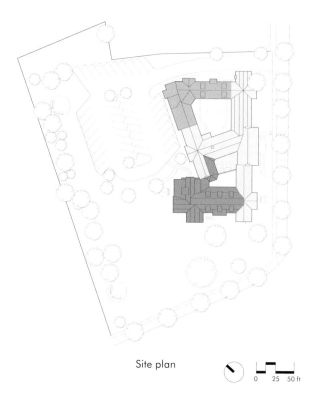

Site plan

0   25   50 ft

18

Left top: Historic Main Street facade of original library building (Aymar Embury II, 1910).

Left middle: The John M. Olin Centennial Addition (Robert A.M. Stern Architects, 1992–1997).

Left bottom: The Arthur and Janet Ross Children's Addition (Robert A.M. Stern Architects, 2001–2014).

Below: View looking south to the children's entry.

Below: View looking
east.

Right: West facade
at dusk.

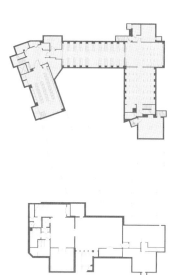

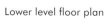

Lower level floor plan

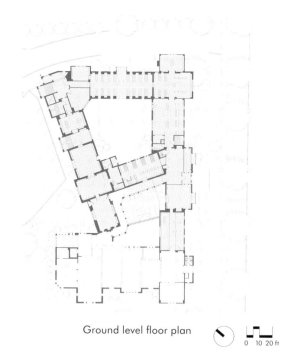

Ground level floor plan

0 10 20 ft

Left: Windmill in the children's reading room.

Top: Information desk.

Bottom: Alcove.

Top: Passage along
west courtyard.

Bottom: Stair to lower
level.

Top: Gallery.

Bottom: The Baldwin Family Lecture Room.

10 Rittenhouse Square

Philadelphia, Pennsylvania
2003–2009
Project Partner:
Graham S. Wyatt

Right: View from
Rittenhouse Square.

This 396-foot-tall, 33-story tower rises behind three historic buildings. Red brick and limestone facades reference the neighborhood's residential character. Generously proportioned high-ceilinged rooms, many with large bay windows, as well as spacious balconies and terraces, open the apartments to views of historic Rittenhouse Square and the Center City skyline.

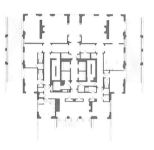

Thirty third floor plan

Twelfth floor plan

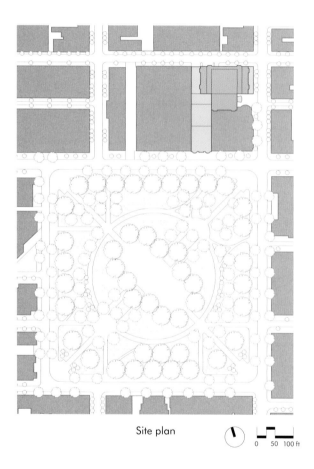

Site plan

0 50 100 ft

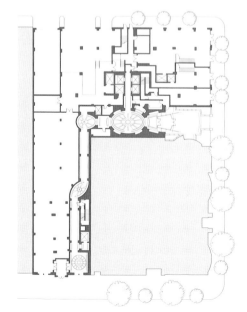

Ground floor plan

0 16 32 ft

East Academic Building

Webster University
Webster Groves, Missouri
2004–2012
Project Partners:
Graham S. Wyatt
Kevin M. Smith

The first building to be built as part of a master plan we prepared to shape a new quadrangle combining existing and new buildings, the East Academic Building is home to the George Herbert Walker School of Business and Technology and other programs that support Webster's signature distance-learning pedagogy and substantial in situ undergraduate and graduate student population.

The limestone-and-red-brick clad, three-story, LEED-Gold building negotiates a 14-foot change in grade with a double-height lobby connecting a first-floor entry at Garden Avenue with a second-floor entrance on the new quad. At the intersection of its two wings, a two-story commons serves as a gathering place. Adjacent to the commons, an open stair links classrooms and seminar rooms with administrative offices. A glass wall at the second-floor gallery commands unobstructed views across the quadrangle to Webster Hall (George Barnett, 1915), the historic centerpiece of the campus.

Site plan

0   50 100 ft

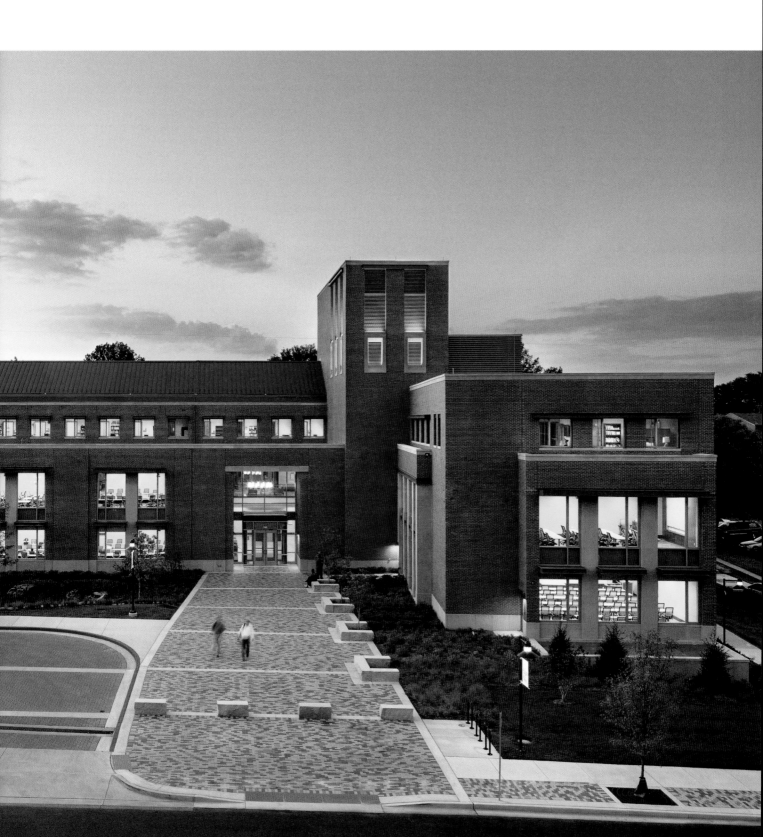

Below: South facade.

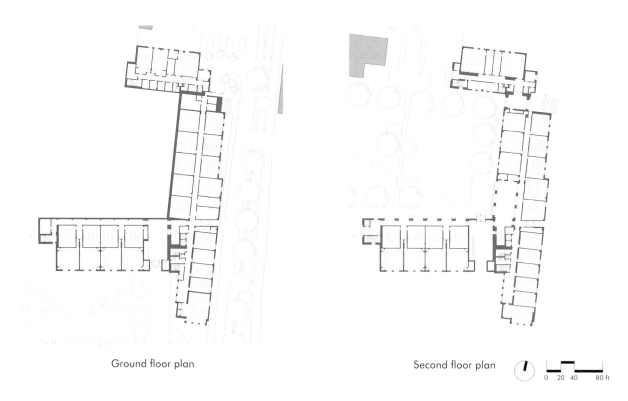

Ground floor plan   Second floor plan

0   20 40   80 ft

Wasserstein Hall, Caspersen Student Center, and Clinical Wing

Harvard Law School
Cambridge, Massachusetts
2004–2012
Project Partners:
Graham S. Wyatt
Melissa DelVecchio
Alexander P. Lamis
Kevin M. Smith

Harvard Law School occupies seventeen disparate buildings, many significant, including the idiosyncratic Austin Hall (H.H. Richardson, 1883), the monumental Langdell Hall (Shepley, Rutan & Coolidge, 1906; Coolidge, Shepley, Bulfinch & Abbott, 1928) and bland graduate student housing (Walter Gropius, 1951). Because its various buildings do not face each other, the Law School lacks a focal space comparable to Harvard Yard; it also lacks a clearly defined point of arrival. To begin to address these conditions, our building is organized in three wings facing the public realm and wrapping an elevated internal courtyard. The academic facilities are housed in the west-facing Wasserstein wing, where a monumental double-height gallery connects the complex's two principal entrances; social spaces are gathered in the Caspersen wing that looks south across the beginnings of a Law School yard made possible by the demolition of one wing of Benjamin Thompson's Pound Hall (1969); clinical offices and conference spaces are located facing the neighborhood to the north.

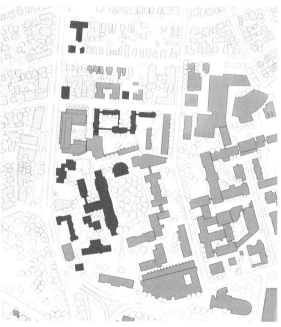

Campus plan

0   250 ft

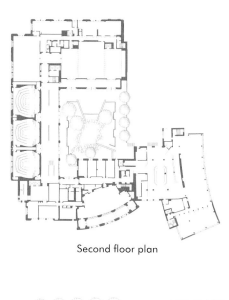

Second floor plan

Fourth floor plan

Ground floor plan

Third floor plan

0 25 50 ft

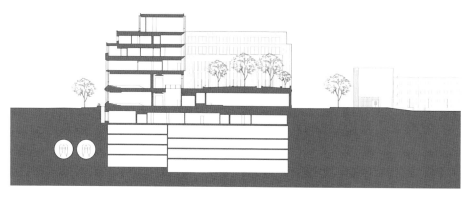

Section

0 16 32 ft

Left: Wasserstein Hall
south entry.

Overleaf: Loggia
at the Caspersen
Student Center.

Top: Second-floor
courtyard.

Bottom: Aerial view
looking northwest.

Top: Wasserstein Hall
lobby.

Bottom: First-floor
gallery and stair.

Right: Second-floor
gallery.

Left: Third-floor lounge in Wasserstein Hall.

Top: Caspersen Student Center lounge.

Bottom: Break-out rooms off first-floor gallery in Wasserstein Hall.

Richard T. Farmer
School of Business

Miami University
Oxford, Ohio
2004 – 2009
Project Partners:
Graham S. Wyatt
Preston J. Gumberich

Facing historic Cook Field on a prominent site at the heart of the campus, at the confluence of the three main roads by which visitors arrive in the rural town of Oxford, the building's three wings define a new south-facing quadrangle anchored by a stand of mature trees, including one majestic sweet gum dating approximately to the university's founding in 1809. In keeping with campus policy, the pavilionated red-brick building is in the Georgian style. A colonnaded porch leads into the double-height Forsythe Commons and adjacent study and dining rooms. A broad skylighted stair atrium connects the below-grade classroom floor to the offices above.

Campus plan

0   500 ft

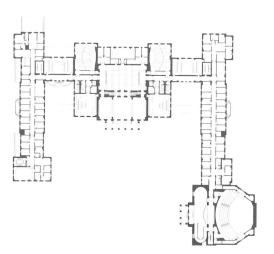

Second floor plan

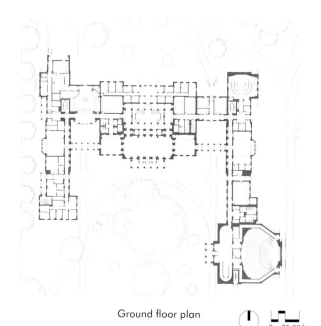

Ground floor plan   0 25 50 ft

Below: View from new quadrangle.

Right top: West facade.

Right bottom: Window bay at west facade.

Left: Forsythe
Commons.

Top: Taylor
Auditorium lobby.

Bottom: Taylor
Auditorium.

Overleaf: Atrium.

49

One Museum Mile

1280 Fifth Avenue
New York, New York
2004–2011
Project Partners:
Paul L. Whalen
Daniel Lobitz

Right: View from
Central Park.

Cradling a plaza on Duke Ellington Circle at the northeast corner of Manhattan's Central Park, this building combines a cultural facility with condominium apartments. Facing the circle on the lower floors, the interiors of the Africa Center—formerly the Museum for African Art—will be designed by others, but our design establishes its identity within the larger whole with distinctive trapezoidal windows and intricate metal screens inspired by African motifs. The facades of the 19-story residential building are composed of rectangular windows set in trapezoidal cast-stone panels, creating a zigzag dimensional relief that carries upward the rhythm of the museum facade and emphasizes the verticality of the tower. Setbacks at the fifth and eleventh floors provide terraces for apartments looking west and south.

Fifth floor plan

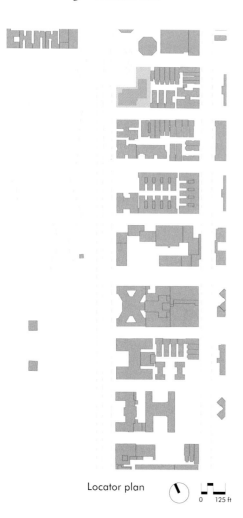

Locator plan   0   125 ft

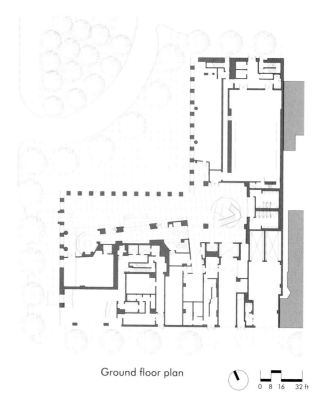

Ground floor plan   0 8 16   32 ft

Left: View looking
south across Duke
Ellington Circle.

Right top: Detail at
south facade.

Right bottom: Detail
at third-floor terrace.

The Century

Los Angeles, California
2004–2010
Project Partners:
Daniel Lobitz
Paul L. Whalen
Sargent C. Gardiner

Set on a four-acre site landscaped to provide an oasis in the midst of the buzz of Century City, this 42-story residential tower welcomes visitors from the Avenue of the Stars along a winding, palm-tree-edged drive leading to a motor court, where a glass canopy leads to a lobby and lounge overlooking terraced gardens.

The tower's elliptical plan provides for a mix of apartments types, each with generously sized balconies to take advantage of open vistas to the Pacific to the west and the San Gabriel Mountains to the east. Fluted columns, protruding eyebrow lintels, and other details inspired by 1930s Moderne architecture establish an atmosphere of casual luxury.

Locator plan

0   200 ft

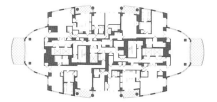

Thirty-seventh floor plan

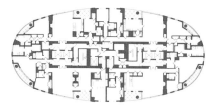

Eleventh to eighteenth floor plans

Ground floor plan

0 10 20   40 ft

Left: Garden terrace.

Top: Lounge.

Bottom: Lobby.

Bavaro Hall

Curry School of Education
University of Virginia
Charlottesville, Virginia
2005–2010
Project Partners:
Graham S. Wyatt
Preston J. Gumberich

While masking the Curry School's Ruffner Hall, an unremarkable 1970s building, from the western perimeter of the red-brick Classicism of the University's historic Central Grounds designed by Thomas Jefferson, Bavaro Hall also defines a landscaped courtyard framed by two open-air arcades. The building's simple massing takes advantage of a steeply sloping site to allow for entrances at grade and at the landing of an existing pedestrian bridge to the main campus.

Campus plan

0   350 ft

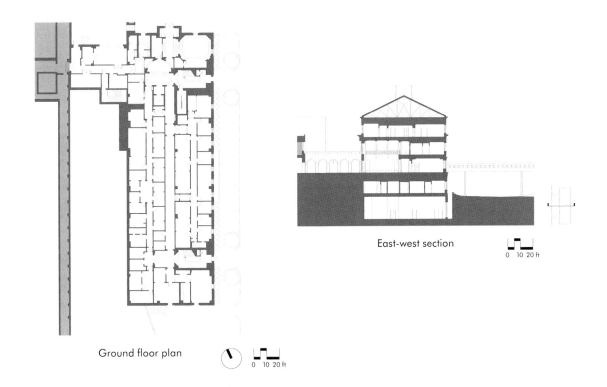

Ground floor plan

0 10 20 ft

East-west section

0 10 20 ft

Top: Commons at
third floor.

Bottom: Commons at
second floor.

Top: Detail at
Commons.

Bottom: Faculty
lounge.

North Hall
and Library

Bronx Community College
The City University of New York
Bronx, New York
2005–2012
Project Partners:
Graham S. Wyatt
Augusta Barone
Alexander P. Lamis

North Hall and Library is the first stylistically sympathetic building added in almost 100 years to the quadrangle Stanford White designed in 1892 for what was originally New York University's University Heights campus. Buff Roman brick and light gray cast-stone trim carry forward the palette of White's buildings. A recessed entry porch leads past an east-west spine of classrooms to a monumental stair rising to a soaring light-flooded reading room, inspired by Henri Labrouste's at the Bibliothèque Ste.-Geneviève in Paris, intended to celebrate learning for commuting students from modest circumstances who seek to further their education while also holding down full-time jobs and caring for families. In another return to tradition, our design embraces a decorative arts program with mural scenes of the Bronx by Daniel Hauben at the main stair landings and on the balcony frieze in the commons, and Greek-key stenciling on the vaulted ceiling by Cid Mendez.

Campus plan

0   200 ft

Second level plan

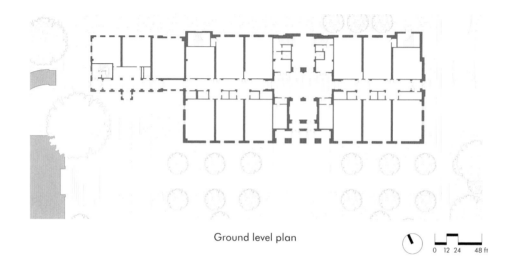

Ground level plan

0 12 24   48 ft

Left: East facade.

Top: View looking west to Philosophy Hall (Stanford White, 1912).

Bottom: View looking east from Philosophy Hall.

Top: Carolyn G.
Williams Reading
Room.

Overleaf: Reading
room balcony.

Bottom: Stair.

Right: Colonettes and
vaulting in reading
room.

Alan B. Miller Hall

Mason School of Business
The College of William and Mary
Williamsburg, Virginia
2005–2009
Project Partners:
Graham S. Wyatt
Kevin M. Smith

Carrying forward the character of William and Mary's long tradition of Georgian-style architecture, Miller Hall is organized around three sides of a landscaped courtyard that opens to the College Woods and the renovated Lake Matoaka amphitheater. A monumental entrance hall connects wings dedicated to the school's graduate and undergraduate programs to a cafe and the Brinkley Commons, which occupies a commanding position on the second floor.

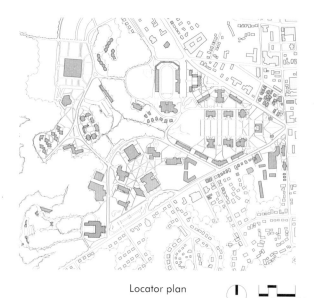

Locator plan

0   300   600 ft

Below: View from
Campus Drive.

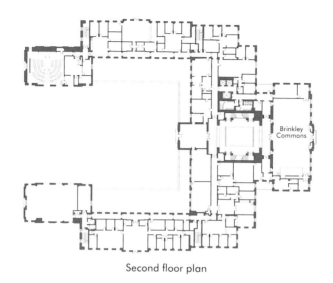

Second floor plan

Ground floor plan

0   20   40 ft

Below: Brinkley
Commons Room
configured for lecture
(top) and dining
(bottom).

Right: Brinkley
Commons Room
entry.

Our Lady of
Mercy Chapel

Salve Regina University
Newport, Rhode Island
2006–2010
Project Partner:
Grant F. Marani

Salve Regina University is located in the heart of Newport's renowned summer cottage district. Set at a campus crossroads, Our Lady of Mercy Chapel is very much in the tradition of New England country churches, here with a Roman Catholic inflection. The building's picturesque massing and Shingle-Style details—sweeping eaves, eyebrow dormers, latticework, local granite—are specific to Newport. The main sanctuary is bathed in natural light from clerestory windows and a high-set oculus, its white-painted walls accented with oak wainscoting, beams, and trusses. In line with evolving liturgical practice, the gently curving pews give worshipers a clear view of their fellow parishioners as well as those who lead the services. An important part of our brief was to display to advantage the generous donation of John LaFarge stained-glass windows salvaged from a nearby private chapel that had been demolished.

Campus plan

0   100   200 ft

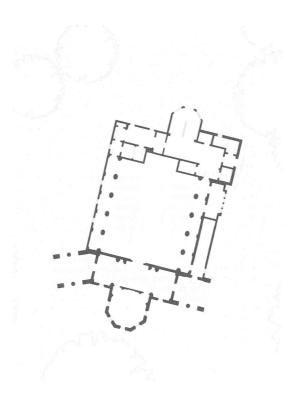

First floor plan

Left: Entry porch.

Top: Chapel.

Bottom: Stained glass windows by John LaFarge in the Rodgers Interfaith Prayer Room.

Overleaf: Chapel.

Superior Ink

New York, New York
2006–2010
Project Partners:
Paul L. Whalen
Michael D. Jones

Right: View from West
Street.

Superior Ink connects two types of buildings that
characterize its West Village neighborhood: a 15-story
residential tower overlooking the Hudson River, with
facades featuring large expanses of glass and metal
detailing inspired by the industrial aesthetic of nearby
warehouses, and seven uniquely designed side-street
townhouses inspired by Colonial and Federal-era
architecture.

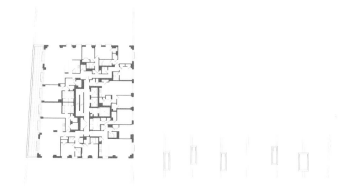

Sixth floor plan

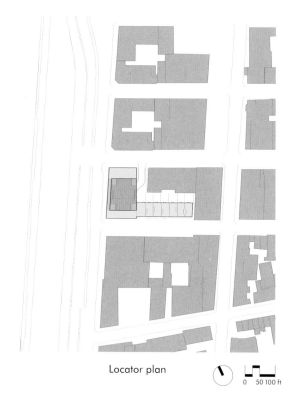

Locator plan   0 50 100 ft

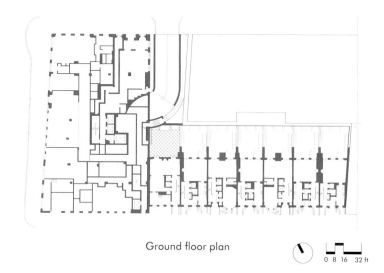

Ground floor plan   0 8 16 32 ft

Below: Tower entry on
West Twelfth Street.

Right: Detail at west
facade.

Christoverson
Humanities Building

Florida Southern College
Lakeland, Florida
2006–2010
Project Partner:
Alexander P. Lamis

Following on the completion of our Barnett
Residential Life Center (2005–2009), we continued
our work on the Frank Lloyd Wright campus with
the Dr. Marcene H. and Robert E. Christoverson
Humanities Building, which provides additional
space for humanities instruction and faculty offices. A
dramatic roof greets visitors approaching along Lake
Hollingsworth Drive. Two sets of stairs rise to a loggia
overlooking Lake Hollingsworth, where a double-
height lounge encourages social interaction among
faculty and students.

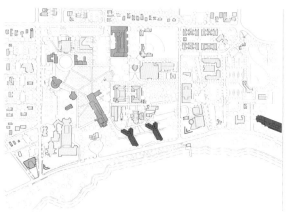

Campus plan

0   300 ft

Left: Stair to loggia.

Below: View looking northwest.

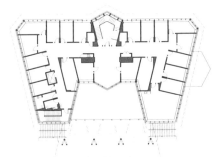

Second floor plan

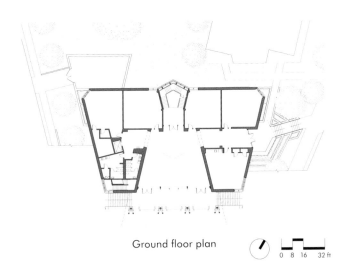

Ground floor plan

0 8 16   32 ft

Left: Detail at loggia.

Right top: Main stair.

Right bottom: Lounge.

North Quad Residential and Academic Complex

University of Michigan
Ann Arbor, Michigan
2006–2010
Project Partners:
Graham S. Wyatt
Preston J. Gumberich

North Quad combines classrooms, offices, meeting rooms, and laboratories for a variety of academic programs with residential suites, dining rooms, and social spaces on a tight urban site where the campus meets the surrounding town. Two L-shaped buildings arranged around interconnected courtyards rise in a counterclockwise spiral to a landmark tower. The early twentieth-century Arts and Crafts work of Emil Lorch, Pond & Pond, and Albert Kahn on the Michigan campus inspired our vocabulary of forms and palette of deep red brick, stone, and slate.

Locator plan

0   280 ft

Below: Dining hall and residential tower at Sprayregen Family Plaza.

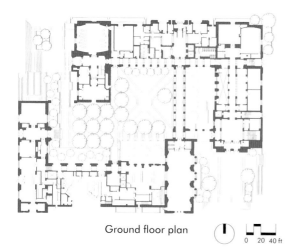

Ground floor plan

0 20 40 ft

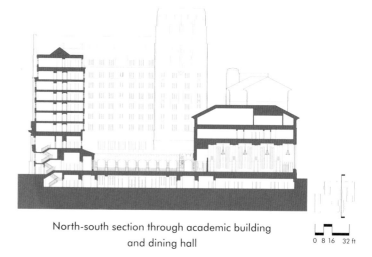

North-south section through academic building and dining hall

0 8 16 32 ft

Left: Entry to residential building at State Street Plaza.

Top: Entry to courtyard at Sprayregen Family Plaza.

Bottom: Courtyard arcade.

Top: Sunken garden.

Bottom: Courtyard.

Right: Arcade.

Top: Benedek Family
Media Gateway
second floor.

Bottom: Detail at
dining hall.

East Hampton
Town Hall

East Hampton, New York
2006–2010
Project Partner:
Randy M. Correll

A collection of eighteenth- and nineteenth-century timber-framed vernacular houses and barns, salvaged by a local couple and then donated to the town, are arranged to serve as a new government campus, accommodating offices and public meeting rooms. Light spills down a stair inside a glass-and-metal conservatory-style lobby that connects the buildings while allowing them to retain their individual integrity. Another historic structure serves as an open-air gateway from adjacent parking.

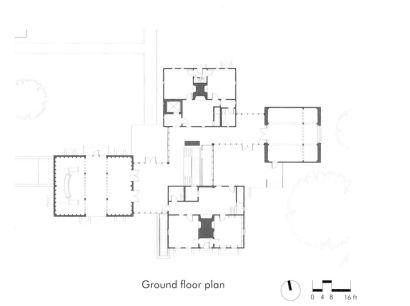

Ground floor plan

0 4 8 16 ft

Stair axonometric

Left: Town Board Meeting Room.

Right top: Reception for the town attorney's office.

Right bottom: Board members' offices.

House in
Sonoma Valley

Glen Ellen, California
2006–2013
Project Partner:
Grant F. Marani

Clients for whom we had designed a house in San Francisco asked us to design a weekend retreat on a property where we'd previously built a guest house and an open-air entertainment pavilion (1999–2006). The massing and palette of the new house—stone, board-and-batten wood siding, exposed cedar rafters, and corrugated metal roofs—are inspired by the regional farm vernacular and the Berkeley Hills cottages of Bernard Maybeck.

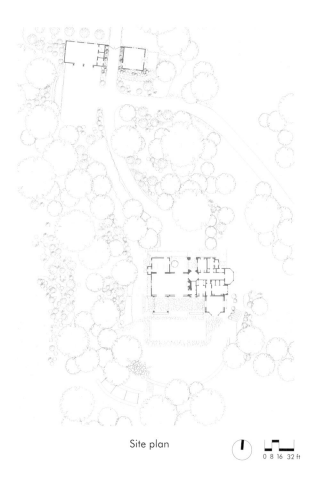

Site plan

0 8 16 32 ft

Below: Aerial view of
main house looking
north.

Left: View from pool
house to guest house.

Right top: Living room
at main house.

Right bottom: Dining
room at main house.

Chapel Hill
Public Library

Chapel Hill, North Carolina
2006–2013
Project Partners:
Alexander P. Lamis
Kevin M. Smith

Two new wings bookend a 1994 library, the north wing providing a new entrance and much-needed community meeting spaces, and the south wing accommodating a generously-proportioned reading room with views to a park. A screen of metal louvers on the south facade shelters the interiors from glare in summer while admitting sunlight deep into the building in winter.

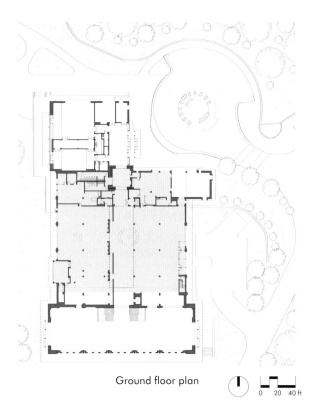

Ground floor plan

0   20   40 ft

136

Below: New south addition.

Left: Detail at east facade.

Below and overleaf: New main reading room.

Mas Fleuri

St.-Jean-Cap-Ferrat, France
2006–2012
Project Partner:
Grant F. Marani

Nestled under a canopy of native umbrella pines, this villa is organized along an axis that leads the eye from a walled entrance court to the sea. Stucco, local limestone, wrought-iron trim, and antique roof tiles reflect the vernacular architecture of nearby hillside villages.

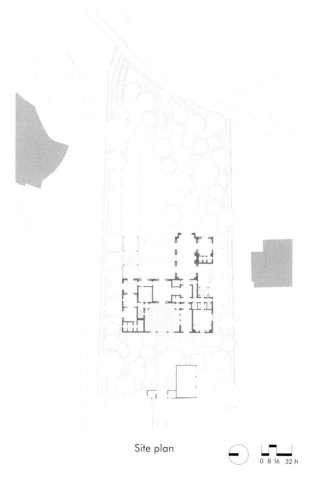

Site plan

0 8 16 32 ft

Left top: Dining
pergola.

Left bottom: View
looking east from
second floor balcony.

Below: View looking
southwest from pool.

Left: Entry arcade
looking west.

Top: Living room.

Bottom: Dining room.

House in Southampton

Southampton, New York
2007–2011
Project Partner:
Randy M. Correll

Replacing a carriage house our clients had lived in for nearly thirty years with the wife's dream of a house that reminds her of childhood summers on the Côte d'Azur, this house consists of a symmetrical two-story main block with single-story wings containing the master suite to the south and the kitchen to the north. The primary rooms face west and relate to a parterre garden that terminates in meadow and woodland.

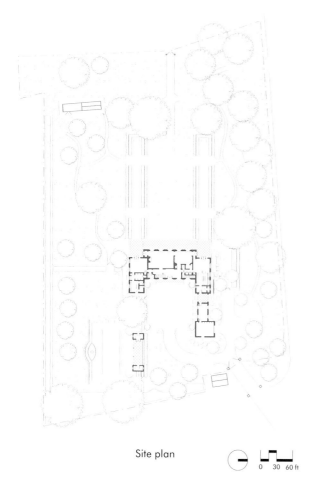

Site plan

0 30 60 ft

Top: Garden (west)
facade.

Bottom: Pool.

Maisonette
in Chicago

Chicago, Illinois
2007–2009
Project Partner:
Randy M. Correll

After 40 years in a house in one of Chicago's northern suburbs, our clients, seeking the convenience of city living, were attracted to a recently-completed maisonette apartment because of its views to Lake Michigan and its direct entry from the street, which provided them with the sense of private domesticity they had been accustomed to for so long. Our task was to reshape the interiors as a sequence of formal rooms for entertaining on the lower floor, with bedrooms above.

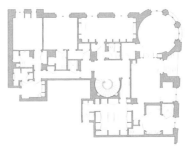

Second floor plan

First floor plan   0 5 10 ft

Top: Study.

Bottom: Library.

18 Gramercy Park

New York, New York
2007–2012
Project Partners:
Paul L. Whalen
Michael D. Jones

Top: Historic photo
from Gramercy Park
c. 1930.

Bottom: Historic
photo of entry
c. 1930.

Right: View from
Gramercy Park.

A 1927 red-brick Georgian building originally designed
by Murgatroyd & Ogden as a dormitory for single
working women, now part of a designated historic
district, was completely reconfigured to create family-
size residences. Within the E-shaped plan of each
full-floor apartment, the living room spans the entire
front of the building facing Gramercy Park to the
north. Adjoining townhouses provide protected diago-
nal views to the park from deep within the building
and allow for ample south light. The building's small
high windows were enlarged while maintaining their
original proportions—a strategy that satisfied the New
York City Landmarks Preservation Commission and
concerned community groups.

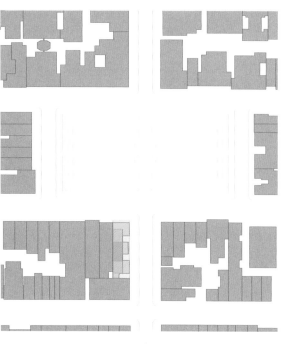

Site plan

0 25 50 100 ft

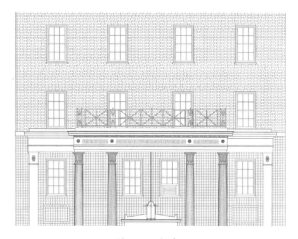

Elevation before

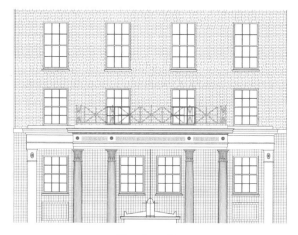

Elevation after

Typical floor plan before

Typical floor plan after

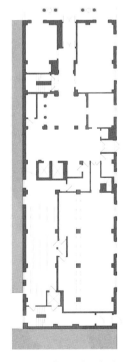

Ground floor plan before

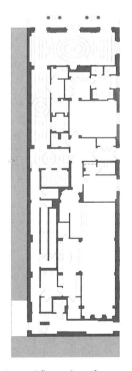

Ground floor plan after

0 4 8   16 ft

161

50 Connaught Road, Central

Hong Kong
2007–2011
Project Partner:
Paul L. Whalen

Below: View looking southwest.

Right: North Facade.

Inspired by 1920s and 1930s office buildings in Hong Kong and Shanghai, and marking a deliberate contrast with Hong Kong's contemporary office towers, 50 Connaught Road stands out with simplified classical detailing rendered in limestone. Large shopfront openings flank a monumental entrance that leads to a 52-foot-high lobby. Windows expressed as triple-height bays enrich the tower's street-facing facade and allow occupants to enjoy commanding views of the harbor. The tower is identifiable by day and at night, when the limestone is washed with light from below.

Twenty-seventh floor plan

Fourth to twenty-first floor plan

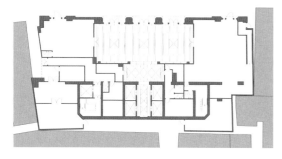

First floor plan

0 2 4 m

50

CONNAUGHT ROAD CENTRAL

Uncommon Charter and Achievement First High Schools

Brooklyn, New York
2007–2010
Project Partners:
Graham S. Wyatt
Augusta Barone
Melissa DelVecchio

Two schools, each designed to serve 800 students, share this six-story building on a mid-block site in Brooklyn's Crown Heights neighborhood. To convey the serious purpose of education, the dignity and civicism that was once part and parcel of New York's public school architecture is evoked on the Pacific Street side with robust classical detailing including three pedimented entrances and oversize window surrounds. To the north, facing Atlantic Avenue, a heavily trafficked commercial thoroughfare, and the elevated tracks of the Long Island Railroad, the design takes on the character of neighboring industrial lofts.

The layout can be easily divided between the two schools, with classrooms on the north side organized around efficient and easily monitored double-loaded corridors; double-height gymnasia are located to the south. A shared rooftop playing field offers impressive views to Manhattan.

Atlantic Avenue

Kingston Avenue

Pacific Street

Site plan

0   100 ft

Below: View looking southwest across Atlantic Avenue.

Left: Entries on Pacific
Street.

Below: View looking
west along Pacific
Street.

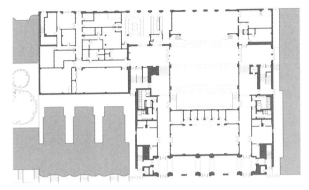

Ground floor plan

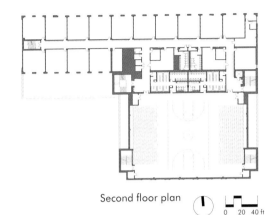

Second floor plan

0 20 40 ft

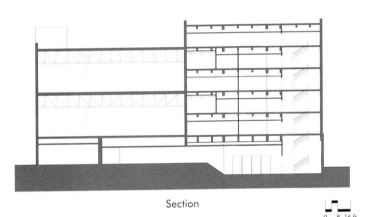

Section

0 8 16 ft

Top: Lobby.

Bottom: Library.

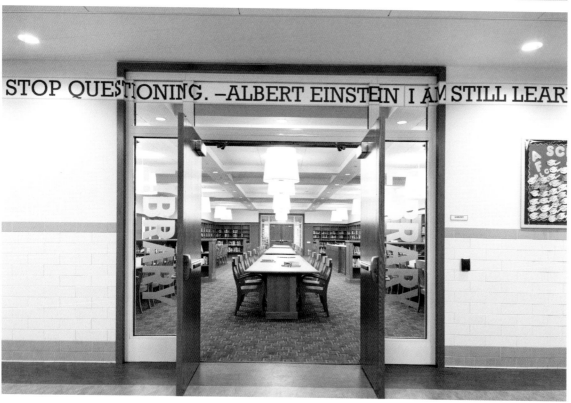

Top: Gymnasium.

Bottom: Cafetorium.

30 Park Place

Four Seasons Private Residences
New York Downtown
New York, New York
Design, 2007–2008; Construction,
2014–2016
Project Partners:
Daniel Lobitz
Paul L. Whalen
Sargent C. Gardiner

Right: View looking
north.

Intended to become a landmark amidst the constella-
tion of tall buildings in Downtown Manhattan, this
slender 82-story, 926-foot tower, combining a luxury
hotel with serviced apartments, occupies the same
block as Cass Gilbert's Woolworth Building (1913).
Notched corners emphasize the tower's verticality as
it rises to a sculpted profile of full-floor penthouses
with setback terraces. Guests will enter the hotel from
Barclay Street; residents have the choice of entrances
from Park Place or from a through-block public garden.

Forty-ninth through fifty-ninth floor plan

Eighth through seventeenth floor plan

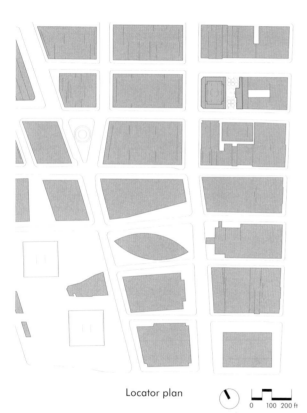

Locator plan

0   100 200 ft

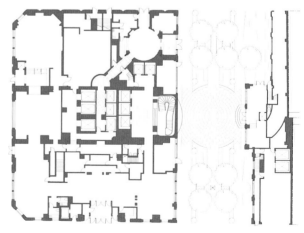

Ground floor plan

0   25 ft

Top: Residential entry.

Bottom: Residential
lobby.

George W. Bush Presidential Center

Southern Methodist University
Dallas, Texas
2007–2013
Project Partners:
Graham S. Wyatt
Alexander P. Lamis
Augusta Barone

Complementing the American Georgian architecture of the Southern Methodist University campus, which it adjoins, this LEED-Platinum brick and limestone building seeks to convey the distinct spirit of an American president and the dignity and power of the presidency itself. A colonnaded plaza welcomes visitors to a pecan-paneled lobby, to one side of which is the library, managed by the National Archives and Records Administration. Straight ahead is Freedom Hall, bathed in diffuse natural light from a 67-foot-high, 50-by-50-foot lantern and from the glow of a 20-foot-high, 360-degree high-definition LED video wall, offering 21st-century versions of traditional narrative murals. Freedom Hall opens to public exhibition galleries, which include a full-scale replica of the Oval Office and a version of the White House Rose Garden as well as to a ceremonial courtyard that can serve both the Library and the Institute.

Entered from the east side of the building, facing SMU, the self-contained George W. Bush Institute includes a 360-seat broadcast-ready auditorium, seminar rooms, and offices on two floors, with a suite of reception rooms and terraces on a third floor overlooking a sustainable native Texas landscape, designed by Michael Van Valkenburgh Associates, and the Dallas skyline.

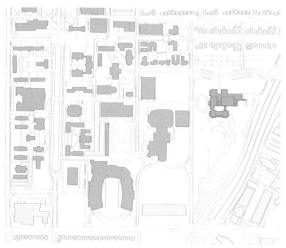

Campus plan

0 250 500 ft

Below: Freedom
Plaza.

Below: North-south
section model.

Right top: South
facade.

Right bottom: View
from park.

Second floor plan

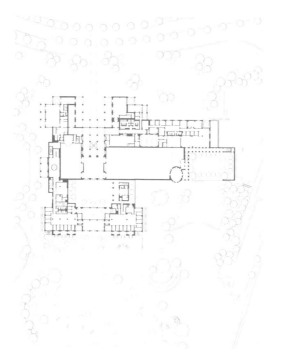

Main floor plan

0   32 64 ft

Left: Institute portico.

Top: Institute entry.

Bottom: View looking southeast.

Top: Detail at oval
office.

Bottom: Freedom
Plaza.

Right: Café 43
terrace.

Left: Freedom Hall.

Right top: Ceremonial courtyard.

Right bottom: Museum lobby.

Top: Typical Institute office.

Bottom: Cross hall.

Right: Institute reading room.

Top: President's office
in the Presidential
Suite.

Bottom: Presidential
Suite reception room.

Tour Carpe Diem

La Défense
Courbevoie, France
2007–2013
Project Partners:
Graham S. Wyatt
Kevin M. Smith
Meghan L. McDermott

Taking an important step forward in the evolution of La Défense toward pedestrian-friendly urbanism, Tour Carpe Diem is the first building oriented both to the raised esplanade—the *dalle* that continues the axis of the Champs-Elysées—and to the urban fabric of the surrounding city of Courbevoie. The 45,500-square-meter, 35-story tower is the first building in France to achieve the double distinction of significantly exceeding the HQE regulations and LEED Platinum certification. It is entered on two levels: from the center of the *dalle* by means of a pedestrian street leading to the building's lobby and to a new monumental public stair connecting the *dalle* and a plaza where a second front facing Boulevard Circulaire welcomes visitors at what was previously very much the back of the site. Double faceted facades, catching the ever-changing Paris light, give the building a strong identity among the towers of La Défense while helping to make explicit the building's dual orientation to the *dalle* and to Courbevoie.

Locator plan

0   50   100 m

Right: View looking
south across
Boulevard Circulaire.

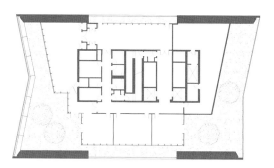

Thirty-fifth floor plan

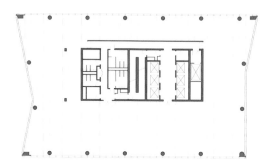

Twenty-fourth floor plan

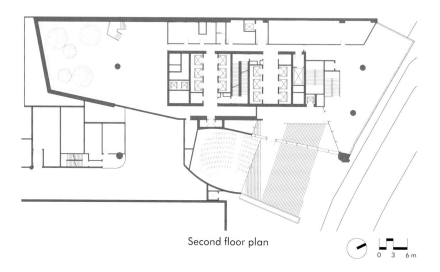

Second floor plan

0   3   6 m

Left: Winter garden.

Right top: Lobby.

Right bottom: Interior
and public stairs.

Below: Roof garden.

Right: View from the *dalle* at dusk.

Hancock Center

Marist College
Poughkeepsie, New York
2007–2011
Project Partners:
Graham S. Wyatt
Kevin M. Smith

On a prominent bluff at the heart of the campus, the new home of Marist's School of Computer Science and Mathematics overlooks the Hudson River and its magnificent valley. Rustic stone walls, red brick window surrounds, and limestone detailing carry forward the quiet Gothic architectural tradition established by the Marist Brothers at the turn of the twentieth century. An L-shaped plan helps to better define two of the campus's green spaces. A tower above the building's main entrance serves as a beacon for the college, visible from the campus gates and from across the river.

Campus plan

0   175   350 ft

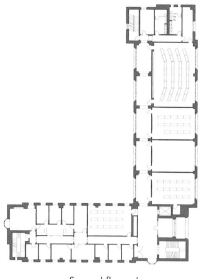

Second floor plan

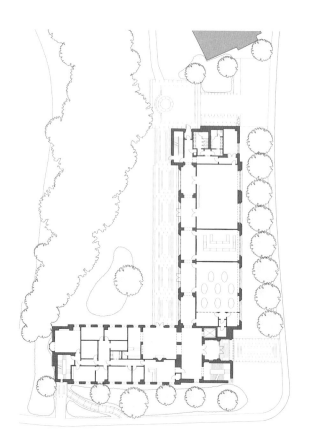

Ground floor plan

0 8 16   32 ft

Left: West terrace.

Top: Lobby.

Bottom: Technology classroom.

Campus Gates and Pedestrian Crossing

Marist College
Poughkeepsie, New York
2009–2011
Project Partners:
Graham S. Wyatt
Kevin M. Smith

North and south campus gates help identify the campus to motorists on heavily-traveled Route 9; the central gate, open only to emergency vehicles, is treated as a lodge in the tradition of the great Hudson Valley estates. Portals inspired by the adjacent Kieran gatehouse, built in 1865, lead to a new pedestrian tunnel under Route 9 to connect the two halves of the campus.

Below: Passage under
Route 9 looking west.

Left: Main gate.

Right top: Detail at main gate.

Right bottom: South gate.

Residence in East Quogue

East Quogue, New York
2008–2013
Project Partner:
Gary L. Brewer

This Shingle-style house on a dune overlooking the Atlantic Ocean offers sweeping views of the water from all major rooms. The gambrel roof, gray-stained fancy-cut shingles, slender Doric columns at the porches, and blue shutters recall earlier shingled houses typical of Eastern Long Island. Inside, an open plan organizes the living room, dining room, and library around a central hall; a living room porch and circular dining porch allow for beachfront entertaining. Upstairs, bedrooms are shaped to fit under the low-slung gambrel roof; below, a game room opens to a sheltered terrace.

Below: Entry (north)
facade at dusk.

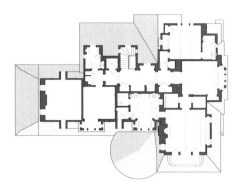

Right top: South
facade.

Right bottom: West
facade at pool deck.

Second floor plan

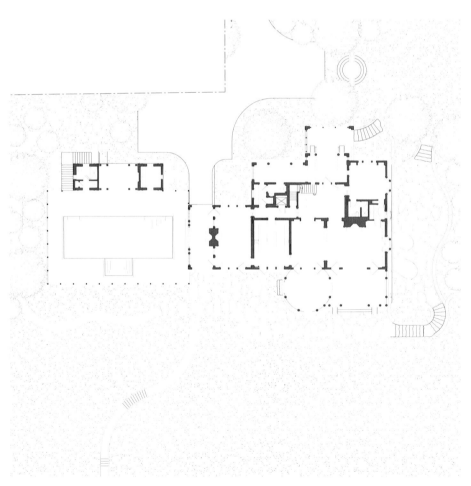

Ground floor plan

0 8 16   32 ft

Below: Dining porch.

Right: Family room.

Overleaf: Living
room.

520 Park Avenue

New York, New York
Design 2008–2009; construction
2014–2017
Project partners:
Paul L. Whalen
Michael D. Jones

Top: View looking
northwest.

Bottom: Aerial view
looking southwest.

A 780-foot-tall, 52-story limestone-clad residential
tower rises to a crown of four corner chimneys framing
pilasters and aedicules where it joins the nearby skyline
of iconic towers such as the Sherry-Netherland and the
Pierre. At street level, the building engages with architecturally distinguished immediate neighbors: Bertram
Goodhue's Grolier Club (1917) and Cram & Ferguson's
Christ Church (1931).

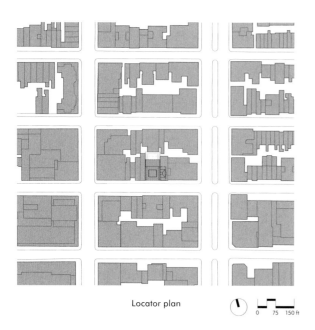

Locator plan

0   75   150 ft

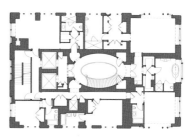

Duplex upper floor

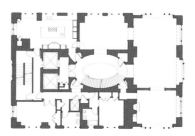

Duplex lower floor

Eighth through fourteenth floor plan

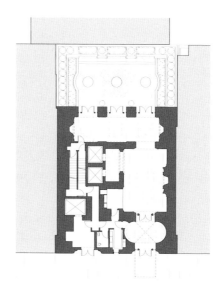

Ground floor plan

0 4 8   16 ft

Axonometric view

0 5 10   20 ft

Below: Lobby.

Right top: Garden.

Right bottom: Pool.

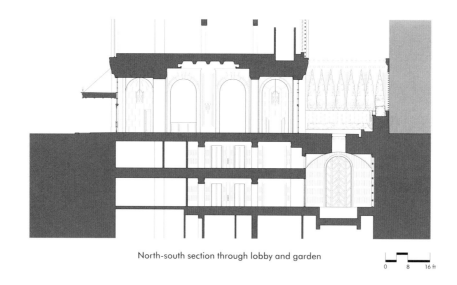

North-south section through lobby and garden

0   8   16 ft

Tiffany Jewel Salon

New York, New York
2008–2010
Project Partner:
Paul L. Whalen

On the mezzanine level of Tiffany's Fifth Avenue flagship, this intimate suite for highly-valued customers deliberately establishes a character distinct from the rest of the store to convey an elegant, glamorous setting in which to view important jewelry collections.

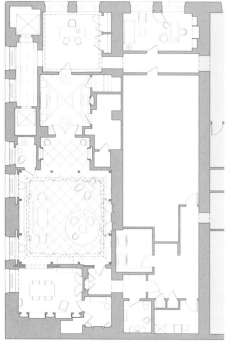

Floor plan

0   5   10 ft

Left: Vestibule looking to salon.

Right top: Atelier.

Right bottom: Salon.

New College House

Franklin & Marshall College
Lancaster, Pennsylvania
2008–2011
Project Partners:
Graham S. Wyatt
Preston J. Gumberich

Set at the northwest corner of campus adjacent to existing athletic fields, on a site bounded on two sides by major public roads, New College House is the first building to be realized as part of a residential quadrangle we proposed early in the life of the project. Housing nearly 200 students in doubles, suites, and apartments, with common spaces on the ground floor opening to a broad west-facing terrace, the four-story building carries forward the Georgian vocabulary established by architect Charles Z. Klauder in the early twentieth century with a palette of red brick, stone, painted wood trim, and slate roofs.

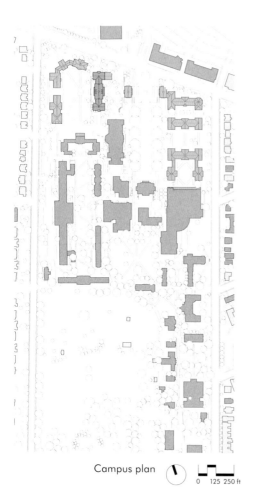

Campus plan

0   125 250 ft

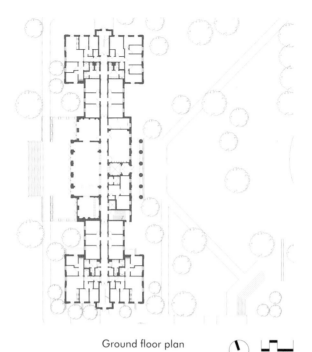

Ground floor plan

0 8 16 32 ft

Below: View looking
southeast.

Right: East entry.

Left: Entry hall.

Top: Lounge.

Bottom: Harkness classroom.

East Campus Master Plan and Caruthers Biotechnology Building

University of Colorado Boulder
Boulder, Colorado
2008–2012
Project Partners:
Paul L. Whalen
Sargent C. Gardiner

Top: Aerial view of main campus.

Bottom: Main campus master plan (Charles Z. Klauder, 1919).

In 2008 we were asked to develop a master plan for CU Boulder's new East Campus, less than half a mile from the school's original campus, designed by architect Charles Z. Klauder, who staggered traditional quadrangles to capture spectacular views to distant mountains while tempering the cold winter winds and hot summer sun. Reflecting Klauder's approach but at the larger scale required for twenty-first-century research laboratory buildings, our plan, also attuned to the dramatic landscape and often harsh weather, calls for the development of pavilionated buildings around a central quadrangle.

Caruthers Biotechnology Building, the first to be realized as part of our plan, defines one side of the planned gateway quadrangle. Laboratories and faculty offices are organized into neighborhoods located in wings arrayed to either side of a central "main street." Landscaped courtyards separate the pavilions. The building's palette of local sandstone, brick, and red barrel-tile roofs echoes the vocabulary of Klauder's buildings on the original campus with asymmetrically pitched roofs in a style that has been described as "Tuscan Vernacular."

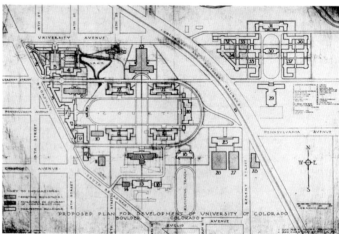

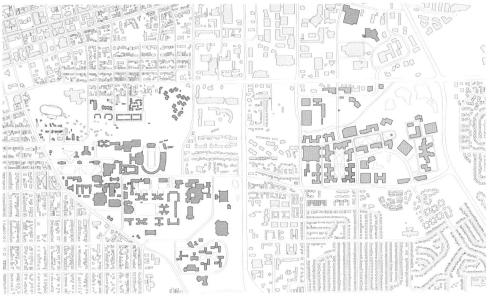

East Campus master plan

0   1300 ft

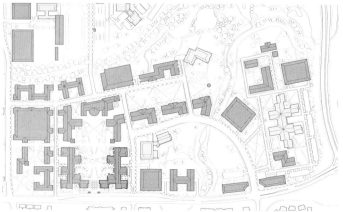

East campus master plan

0   400 ft

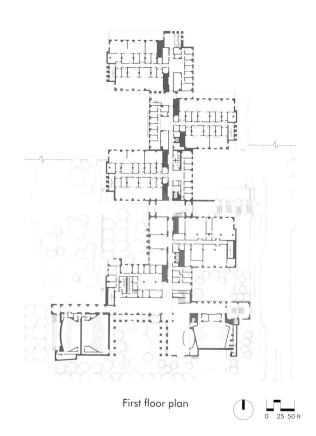

First floor plan

0 25 50 ft

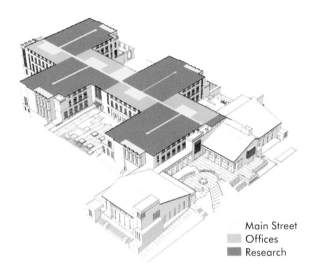

Neighborhood diagram

Main Street
Offices
Research

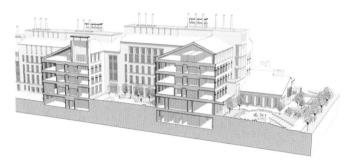

Section perspective

Left: View looking
northwest.

Right top: South
terrace.

Right bottom: South
courtyard.

House on
Hook Pond

East Hampton, New York
2008–2010
Project Partner:
Randy M. Correll

To breathe new life into a modest house that had long
served as home and studio for a couple who were both
artists, without sacrificing its casual character, what
had been the living room was converted into a master
suite, while the studio, retaining its simple finishes and
the artists' work table and easels, became the living
room. An adjacent two-car garage was replaced by an
abstractly-massed studio-like two-story guest wing
with large windows and an angular profile.

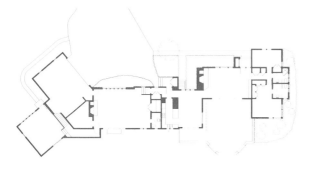

Ground floor plan before

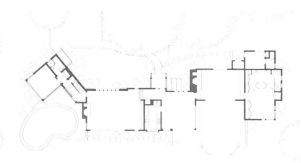

Ground floor plan after

0   10   20 ft

Top: View looking
southeast.

Bottom: Pool.

Residential Colleges 13 and 14

Yale University
New Haven, Connecticut
Design 2008–2010; construction
anticipated 2015–2017
Project Partners:
Graham S. Wyatt
Melissa DelVecchio

Below: South college
master's house.

Right: North college
main courtyard
looking north.

Yale's system of residential colleges, a cornerstone of its undergraduate experience, was established in the 1930s, with four of them designed by James Gamble Rogers (1867–1947) in the Gothic style to complement his other buildings for the University, including the Law School and the Sterling Memorial Library. Our two new colleges, accommodating a total of 900 students, are organized on the traditional entryway system that supports a sense of community within the larger whole. Fraternal twins separated by a landscaped public walk, the colleges are similar in size and palette but each with a distinct plan, variously-sized courtyards, dining halls, libraries, masters' houses, and towers.

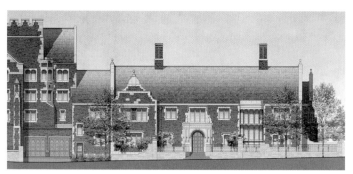

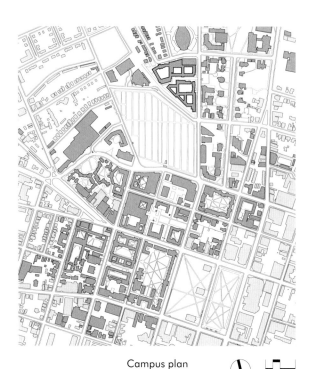

Campus plan

0   400 ft

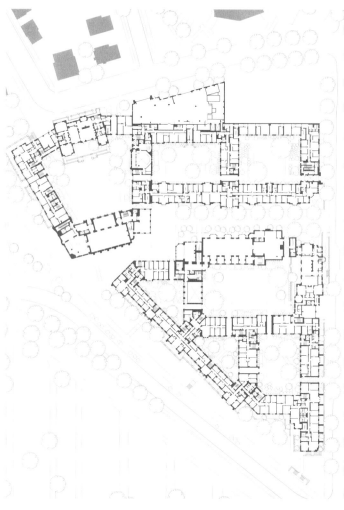

Ground floor plan

0   32   64 ft

Left: View from
Prospect Walk
looking west.

Below: View from
Farmington Canal
Trail looking north.

Left: North college dining hall.

Right top: South college library.

Right bottom: North college library.

Stayer Center for Executive Education

Mendoza College of Business
University of Notre Dame
Notre Dame, Indiana
2008–2013
Project Partners:
Graham S. Wyatt
Melissa DelVecchio
Preston J. Gumberich

Constituting a southern campus gateway, our building is organized by an H-shaped plan to facilitate multiple connections to Notre Dame's classically organized but predominantly Gothic campus. Two floors linked by a south-facing double-height gallery help unite a multi-purpose room, classrooms, and a chapel. An executive lounge on the third floor is located to command views to the iconic gold dome of the University's Main Building (Willoughby J. Edbrooke, 1879).

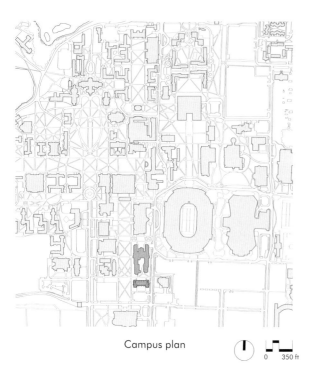

Campus plan

0   350 ft

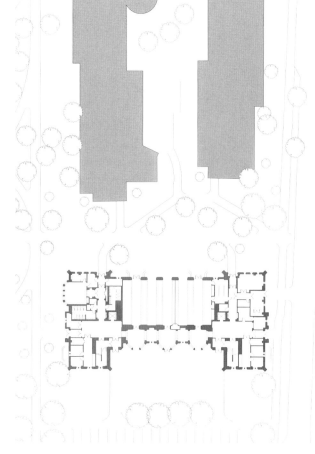

Below: View looking east to the Mendoza College of Business complex.

Right: View looking southwest.

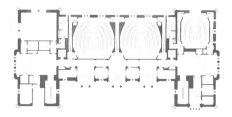

Ground floor plan

Second floor plan

0 8 16 32 ft

Below: East entry.

Right: South entry.

Product Design

2010–2014
Project Partners:
Alexander P. Lamis
Daniel Lobitz

Top: Beekman wing chair for Kindel.

Left bottom: Tracery Collection fabric for Stinson.

Right bottom: Light Play Collection fabric for Stinson.

A suite of furniture for Kindel scaled for contemporary living updates American precedents with clean lines and elegant detailing. Outdoor furniture for Landscape Forms looks to the traditions of American civic street amenities; the urbanity of pre-War New York apartment houses inspired our Avenue doors for Lualdi, nineteenth-century French precedents are stripped to their essence and expressed in crisp, sinuous metal forms for door hardware by SA Baxter, and in floating planes of glass suspended from slender brasswork for lighting by Remains. Ceramic tiles for Walker Zanger, playful interpretations of architectural patterns, include large-scale classical pilasters. Fabrics for Stinson and coordinated carpets for Bentley are inspired by the play of light and shadow on architectural elements. Our collaboration with David Edward continues with an executive chair; and a cast-stone mantelpiece for Haddonstone complements our collection of garden ornaments.

Top: Light Play Collection fabric for Stinson and carpet for Bentley.

Left bottom: Melville bench for Landscape Forms.

Right bottom: Alcott light for Landscape Forms.

Left: Avenue doors for
Lualdi.

Right top: High
Wine chandelier for
Remains Lighting.

Right bottom: Aegean
tile for Walker Zanger.

Left top: Classic fireplace for Haddonstone.

Right top: Flourish Collection hardware for SA Baxter.

Left bottom: Stuyvesant armchair and Butterfield table for Kindel.

Right middle: Robert A.M. Stern Collection hardware for SA Baxter.

Right bottom: Executive chair for David Edward.

Fitness and Aquatics Center

Brown University
Providence, Rhode Island
2009–2012
Project Partner:
Gary L. Brewer

Framing the new Ittleson Quadrangle, this building brings the character of Brown's traditional brick buildings to the northeastern edge of the campus while also acknowledging Providence's tradition of robustly Classical industrial buildings. The Nelson Fitness Center forms a head-house facing Hope Street; the Zucconi Varsity Strength and Conditioning Center faces the playing fields to the east; bracketed between them is the Katherine Moran Coleman Aquatics Center, accommodating a 56-meter swimming pool set one level below grade to reduce its apparent mass.

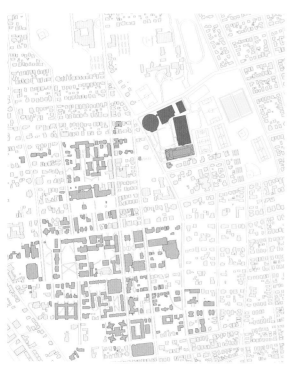

Campus plan

0   300 600 ft

274

Left: Nelson Fitness
Center west facade.

Below: Zucconi
Varsity Strength and
Conditioning Center
east facade.

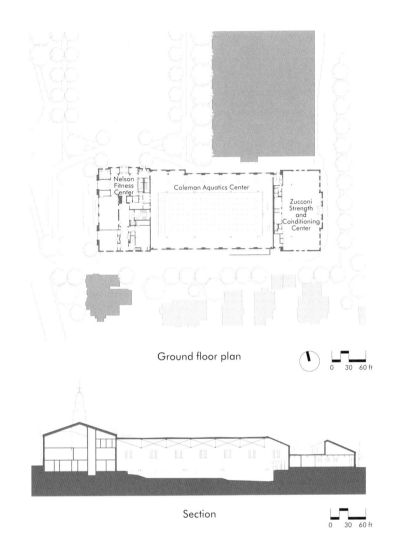

Ground floor plan

0 30 60 ft

Section

0 30 60 ft

Left top: Nelson
Fitness Center lobby.

Left bottom: Nelson
Fitness Center
exercise loft.

Below: Katherine
Moran Coleman
Aquatics Center.

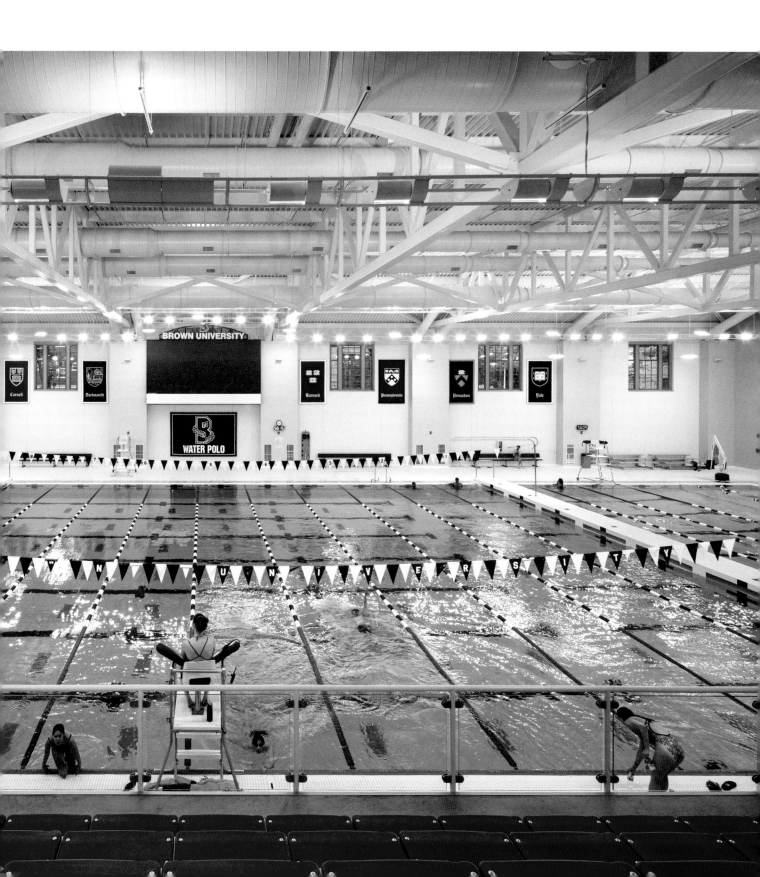

Kohler Environmental Center

Choate Rosemary Hall
Wallingford, Connecticut
2009–2012
Project Partners:
Graham S. Wyatt
Kevin M. Smith

Some schools build environmentally responsible buildings; some schools teach environmental responsibility. The Kohler Environmental Center, located on a spacious site a short bike ride from the Choate Rosemary Hall campus, brings these two objectives together, accommodating cohorts of up to twenty students who board and take their classes at the LEED-Platinum, net-zero facility, and by monitoring and influencing the building's energy use, teach themselves important lessons about how to live sustainably and responsibly.

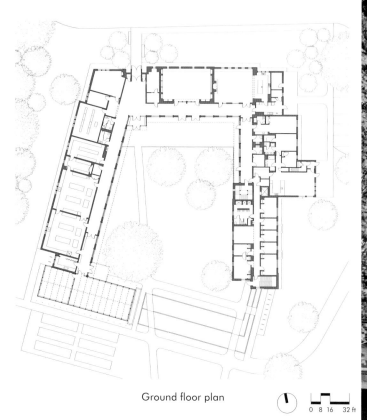

Ground floor plan

0 8 16 32 ft

Top left: Geothermal heating and cooling.

Top right: Natural light.

Middle left: Natural ventilation.

Middle right: Solar hot water.

Bottom: North facade.

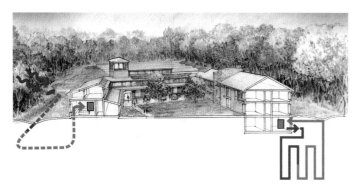

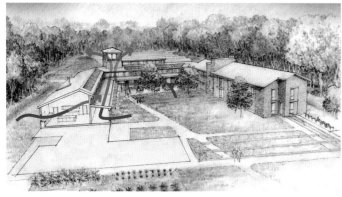

Left: Gallery at entry.

Top: Lounge.

Bottom: Teaching lab.

Heart of Lake

Xiamen, China
2009–2018
Project Partners:
Grant F. Marani
Paul L. Whalen
Sargent C. Gardiner
Michael D. Jones

Inspired by the combination of European-style buildings and Chinese vernacular urbanism at nearby Gulong Island, a historic European Treaty Port, Heart of Lake, occupying the tip of a peninsula bounded by a public waterfront park, is a fully pedestrian garden enclave accommodating 800 families. Local Yellow Rust granite clads residential buildings at multiple scales ranging from individual villas to tall apartment towers. Below-grade parking for 1,650 cars frees up the site for a network of pedestrian streets and a generous central park. The project is being implemented in eight phases: construction began in 2012, and the first three phases, including the gateway clubhouse, have been completed; as construction continues, we are now taking up the design of phase 7.

Master plan

0   40 m

Below: View looking east to residential towers.

Overleaf left: Aerial view looking west.

Overleaf right: View from entry drive.

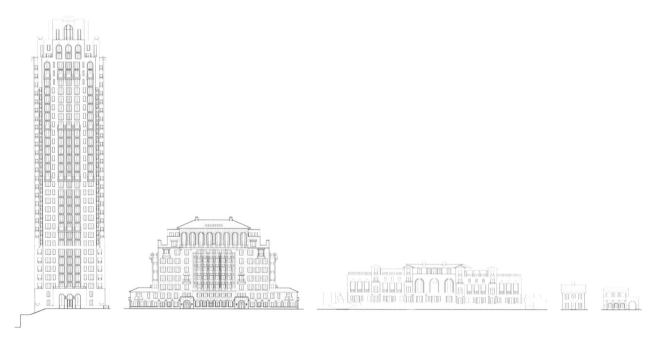

HIGH-RISE   MID-RISE   VILLA   TOWNHOUSE MAISONETTE

Left: Grand stair.

Right top: Courtyard.

Right bottom: Path between private gardens.

Top: Clubhouse south facade.

Bottom: Clubhouse entry.

Right: View of clubhouse courtyard from terrace.

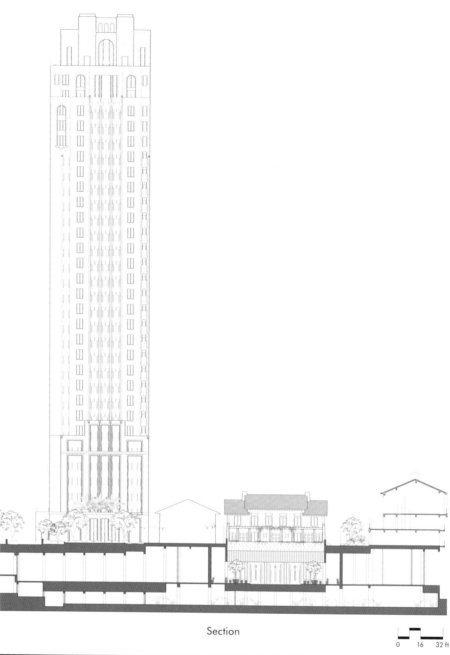

Section

0   16   32 ft

Left: Clubhouse
reception hall.

Below: Clubhouse
rotunda.

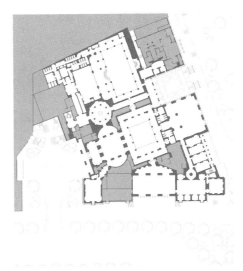

Ground floor plan

0   10   20 m

Gerri C. LeBow Hall

LeBow College of Business
Drexel University
Philadelphia, Pennsylvania
2009–2013
Project Partners:
Graham S. Wyatt
Kevin M. Smith

Below: East facade
from Market Street
and 32nd Street.

Right: View looking
southeast across
Market Street.

Marking the intersection of Woodland Walk and
Market Street, a key gateway to the Drexel campus
from Center City and Thirtieth Street Station, this
twelve-story building can be entered at its three corners. Social spaces are grouped around a central atrium
in which a dramatic suspended stair rises from a below-
grade auditorium to a fourth-floor conference center.
To achieve greater transparency for the social spaces
from the street and the quad, an aluminum and glass
curtainwall wraps the building's lower floors; the tower
above is clad in Indiana limestone.

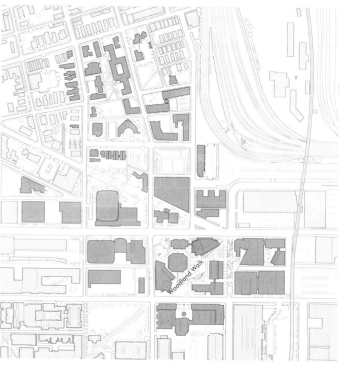

Campus plan

0   150 300 ft

Eighth through eleventh floor plan

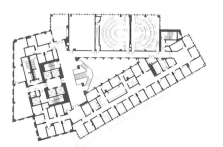

Fourth floor plan

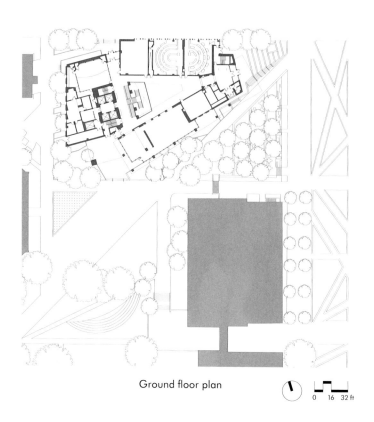

Ground floor plan

0 16 32 ft

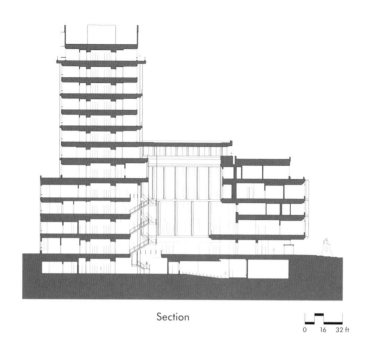

Section

0   16   32 ft

Chestnut Square

Drexel University
Philadelphia, Pennsylvania
2010–2013
Project Partners:
Graham S. Wyatt
Kevin M. Smith

Chestnut Square combines an 18-story residential tower of two- and four-bedroom flats for Drexel students with two six-story "liner" buildings that offer a choice of two- and four-bedroom duplex suites, with living rooms and kitchens at the entry levels and bedrooms alternately above and below. Forming the south edge of Drexel's new quadrangle, the "liner" buildings cantilever toward each other to frame a view to the Mandell Theater (1973) and provide access through a new glass rotunda to existing below-grade dining.

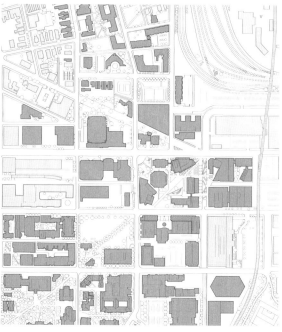

Campus plan

0   300 ft

Below: View looking east across Mandell Courtyard.

Right: Pavilion connecting plaza to Handschumacher Dining Center.

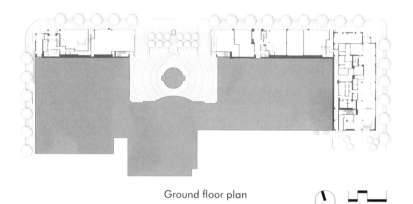

Ground floor plan

0   32   64 ft

Left: View looking
southwest from
Chestnut Street and
32nd Street.

Below: Residential
suite.

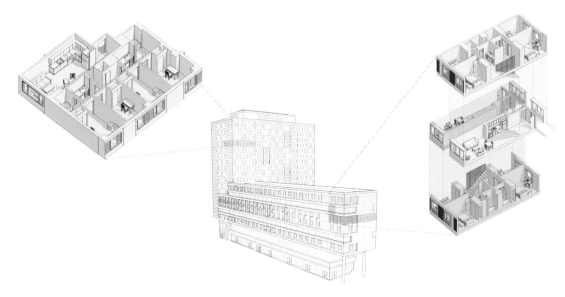

Diagram showing simplex apartment in the tower
and duplex residential suites in the liner building.

Cedarwoods

Willimantic, Connecticut
2009–2012
Project Partner:
Grant F. Marani

Common Ground, a non-profit organization dedicated to ending homelessness, asked us to design a 60-apartment affordable housing development for which the basic program and massing had already been established. On a 20-acre site, half of which is set aside as natural wetlands, we grouped the three three-story wings around a crescent-shaped motor court in the manner of a rambling New England inn, with connecting octagonal hinges on each floor serving as shared social spaces.

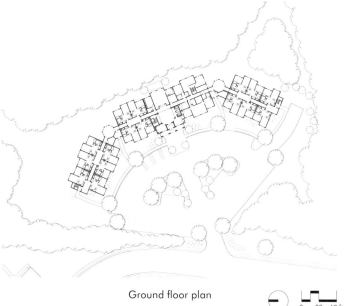

Ground floor plan

0   30   60 ft

L. William
Seidman Center

Seidman College of Business
Grand Valley State University
Grand Rapids, Michigan
2009–2013
Project Partners:
Graham S. Wyatt
Preston J. Gumberich

Prominently located on the west bank of the Grand
River, the buff-colored Norman brick and stone building, with its low-pitched, deep overhanging roofs, refers
back to the Prairie-style architecture of the Midwest
and to the design of key buildings at the University.
Above an arched western entrance, a 122-foot stone,
brick, and glass tower serves as a beacon for the College
and for the campus, visible from across the river and
from the nearby elevated freeway. An S-shaped plan
embraces both a street-facing courtyard and one opening to the city's beloved river walk.

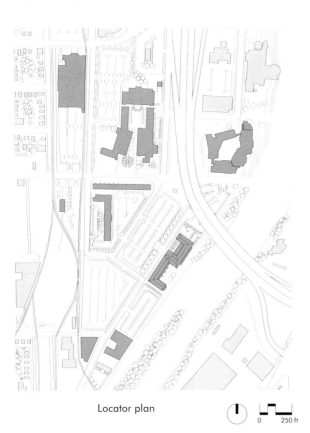

Locator plan

0   250 ft

Second floor plan

Below: View looking
northwest from the
Grand River.

Right: North
courtyard.

Overleaf: South
courtyard.

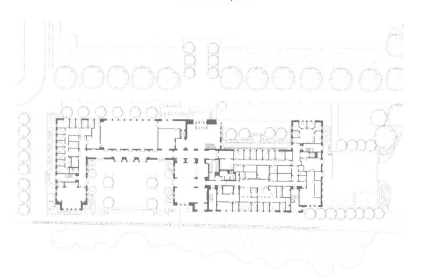

Ground floor plan

0 16 32   64 ft

Left: The Frey
Foundation lobby.

Top: Student lounge.

Bottom: South
gallery.

House on Georgica Pond

East Hampton, New York
2009–2013
Project Partner:
Randy M. Correll

Top: View from entry drive (before).

Bottom: View from entry drive (after).

Right: Entry (north) facade.

Overleaf: View looking northwest across Georgica Pond.

To expand a Shingle-style residence that the owners had built twenty years earlier while preserving its original character, the roof between two disconnected gambrels on the entry facade was raised and the service wing and garage were integrated into the main mass. The L-shaped plan orients the primary rooms to water views through expansive new picture windows and French doors opening to a continuous covered porch.

Ground floor plan before

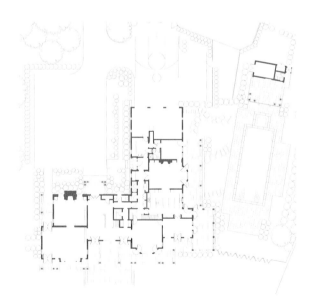

Ground floor plan after

0 10 20 ft

Top: South porch.

Bottom: Pool pavilion.

Residence on Nassim Road

Singapore
2010–2014
Project Partners:
Grant F. Marani
Paul L. Whalen

Below: Construction
view of north facade.

White stucco walls, sandstone quoining, dark green half-timbering, and deep eaves interpret Singapore's highly admired Black-and-White Bungalow style, a local variant of English Arts-and-Crafts. The front entrance leads from the cobblestone motor court through a rotunda to a courtyard wrapped in covered loggias that provide shade and cross-ventilation to temper the tropical climate. A swimming pool terrace is cradled between the living room wing and a guest house.

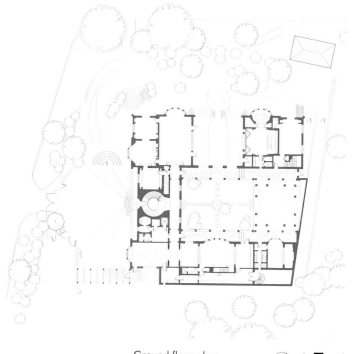

Ground floor plan

0   15   30 m

Farrell Hall

Wake Forest Schools of Business
Wake Forest University
Winston-Salem, North Carolina
2010–2013
Project Partners:
Graham S. Wyatt
Kevin M. Smith

Uniting previously scattered programs, Farrell Hall is the first of a second ring of buildings intended to extend Jens Frederick Larson's 1956 campus plan. Simple Georgian facades, consistent with Larson's designs, address the campus core, but to the west a dramatic curving window wall opens the triple-height balconied Founders Living Room to a loggia, terrace, and lawn shaded by a grove of mature pin oaks. A cockpit-like projecting double-height colloquium room at the third floor accommodates both formal and informal events, while a 350-seat auditorium shares the lower level with six large classrooms.

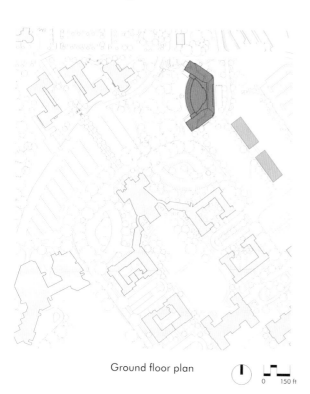

Ground floor plan

0   150 ft

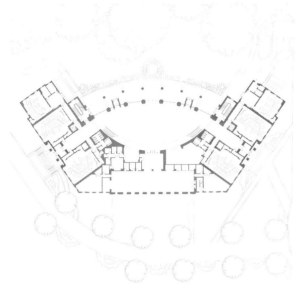

Ground floor plan

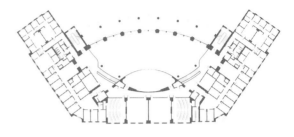

Third floor plan

0   20 40 ft

Below: View looking
southeast.

Overleaf: Founders
Living Room.

Right top: Reynolds
American Foundation
Terrace.

Right bottom: View
looking east.

THE JOHN MEDLIN COMMONS

FOUNDERS LIVING ROOM

Top: Founders Living Room looking west.

Bottom: Founders Living Room looking east.

Right: View of Bern Beatty Colloquium from Founders Living Room.

Left: Bern Beatty
Colloquium.

Top: Cluster
classroom.

Bottom: Broyhill
Auditorium.

Ozark Hall

University of Arkansas
Fayetteville, Arkansas
2010–2013
Project Partner:
Gary L. Brewer

Our work at Ozark Hall combined the restoration of the facades and interiors of a 1940s building and the completion of its originally envisioned U-shaped plan with a new wing to provide the Honors College with lounges, offices, and an auditorium tucked into the sloping site. The new wing is faithful to the characteristic trapezoidal stonework and ornament of the Collegiate Gothic architecture established on the campus by Jamieson & Spearl in the 1920s.

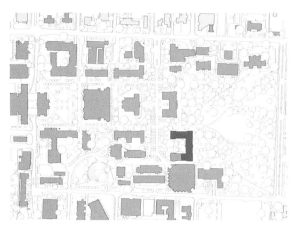

Campus plan

0   250 ft

Below: Restored east facade.

Right: View of new wing from courtyard.

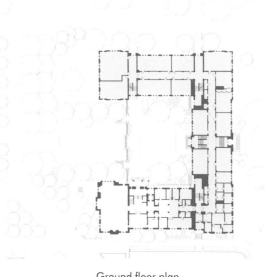
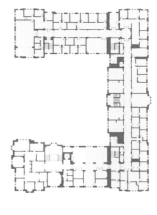

Ground floor plan

Second floor plan

0 16 32 ft

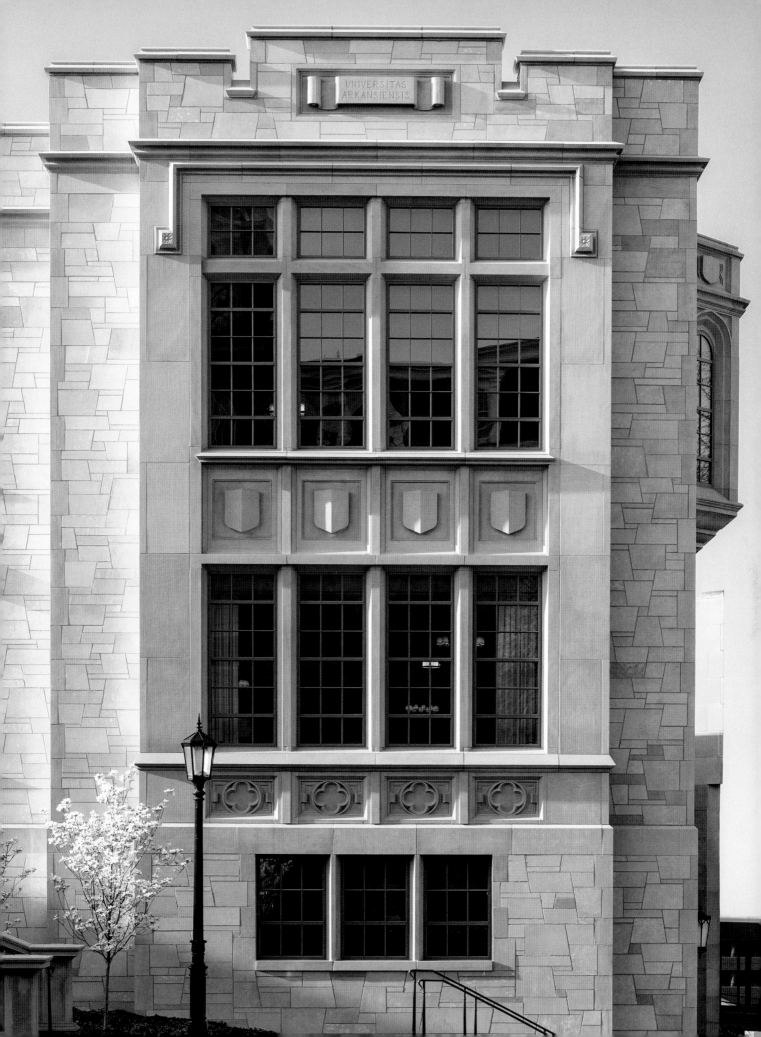

Top: Stair hall.

Bottom: Second floor
lounge.

Residential Tower at Xinyi

Taipei, Taiwan
2010–2015
Project Partners:
Paul L. Whalen
Michael D. Jones

Left: Construction view.

Right: View looking northwest.

A robust vocabulary of pilasters, cornices, columns, and loggias reflecting New York's early twentieth-century luxury townhouses and apartment buildings, as well as Taipei's own tradition of Western Classicism, characterizes this 22-story, 90-meter-high granite-clad apartment tower, now under construction. The tower is accessed across a stone-paved motor court. A residential library opens to an Italianate garden with fountains.

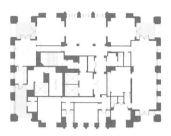

Tenth to nineteenth typical floor plan

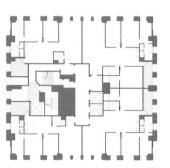

Second to sixth typical floor plan

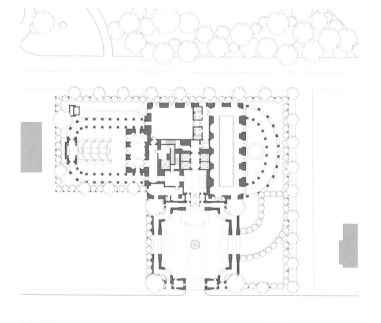

Ground floor plan

0   5   10 m

Abington House on the High Line

New York, New York
2010–2014
Project Partners:
Daniel Lobitz
Paul L. Whalen

Right: View looking
north along the High
Line.

Rising at the dramatic point where the north-south
stretch of New York's High Line veers west to the
Hudson River, this 33-story, 312-unit rental apartment tower, with its robust detailing—metal casement
windows and black metal-framed panels of variegated
brick with black-glazed brick accents—is inspired
by the structure of the High Line itself and by the
industrial character that first attracted people to the
neighborhood. Storefronts on Tenth Avenue and West
30th Street connect the building directly to city life;
a south-facing garden court and entry drive that runs
under the High Line serves an oasis of quiet, a theme
carried forward in the building's public spaces.

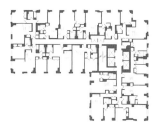

Seventh through sixteenth floor plan

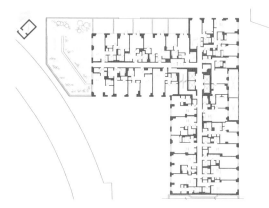

Third floor plan

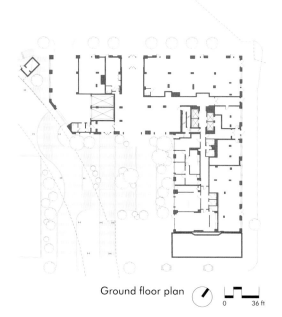

Ground floor plan

Locator plan

0   300 ft

0   36 ft

Left: Details at west facade.

Right: Detail view looking southwest over the High Line.

Navy Yard
Master Plan Update

Philadelphia, Pennsylvania
2013
Project Partners:
Graham S. Wyatt
Meghan L. McDermott

Top: Mustin Park District.

Middle: Canal District.

Bottom: Aerial view from the Delaware River.

Building on the success of our 2004 plan for the redevelopment of the Philadelphia Navy Yard, our 2013 update reinforces the Historic Core neighborhood as the plan's "downtown" with new apartment buildings added to the mix of new and historic office buildings, many devoted to education and research. Attention is drawn to the development potential of the Delaware River front by proposing two new office districts, a seven-acre park, and a canal. At full build-out, the Navy Yard will support up to 13.5 million square feet of development, 30,000 people, and over $3 billion in private investment.

2004 Master plan

0   1000 ft

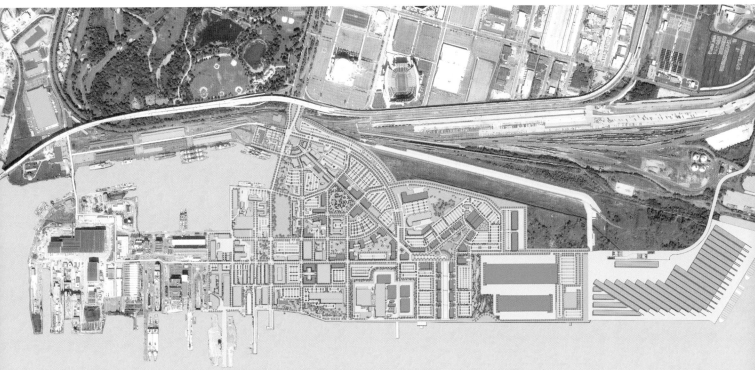

Master plan

0   500 1000 ft

5 Crescent Drive

The Navy Yard
Philadelphia, Pennsylvania
2010–2013
Project Partners:
Graham S. Wyatt
Meghan L. McDermott

A dynamic 21st-century workplace for the North American operations of leading international pharmaceutical company GlaxoSmithKline features unassigned seating rather than private offices or cubicles, encouraging employees to work at locations best suited to the tasks at hand each day. A winter garden is treated as an internal street lined with employee services such as a restaurant and a company store. Crisscrossed by translucent walkway bridges and punctuated by a dramatic spiraling stair, the street is intended to provide opportunities for chance encounters and the exchange of ideas among employees.

Locator plan

0   1000 ft

Left: View looking southeast from Crescent Park.

Below: View looking southeast across Crescent Drive.

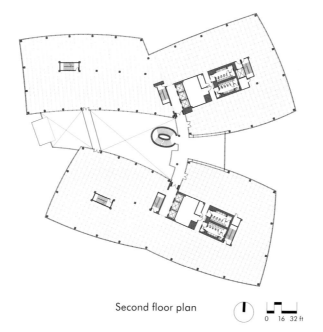

Second floor plan

0   16   32 ft

Ground floor plan

0   16   32   64 ft

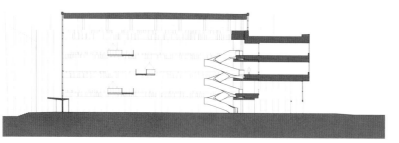

East-west section through atrium

0   16   32 ft

Left: Spiral stair.

Below: Walkways in atrium.

Immanuel Chapel

Virginia Theological Seminary
Alexandria, Virginia
2011–2015
Project Partner:
Grant F. Marani

Below: Construction
view looking
northeast.

Replacing but not emulating an 1881 Victorian Gothic chapel lost to fire in 2010, Immanuel Chapel instead reflects the understated red-brick Georgian of the Seminary's more typical buildings, while counterpointing the rich Italianate tower of its oldest building, nearby Aspinwall Hall (1859). Together with a Welcome Center, Immanuel Chapel will form for the first time a visible gateway to the campus from Seminary Road, inviting members of the surrounding community to join seminarians in worship and learning. The cruciform shape of the vaulted sanctuary is intended to provide a flexible worship space bathed in indirect light from the large ambulatory windows.

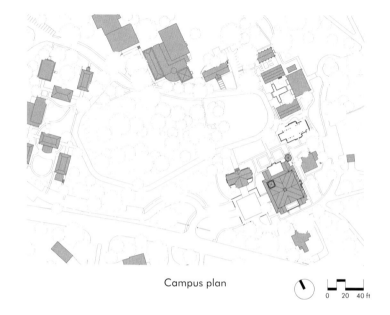

Campus plan

0 20 40 ft

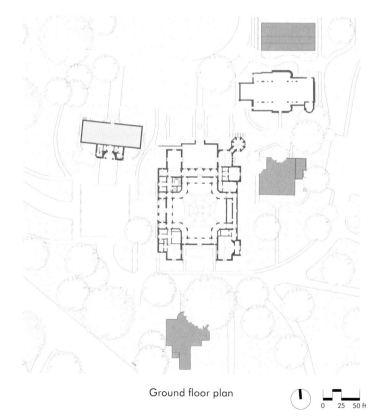

Ground floor plan

0 25 50 ft

Site section looking east

0   16   32 ft

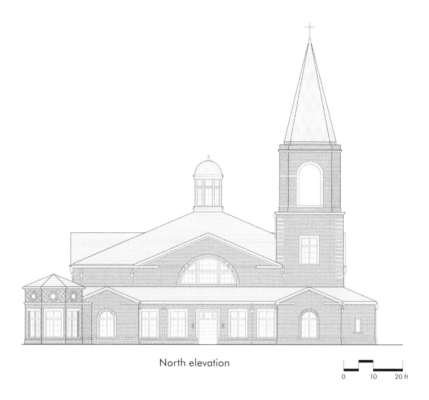

North elevation

0   10   20 ft

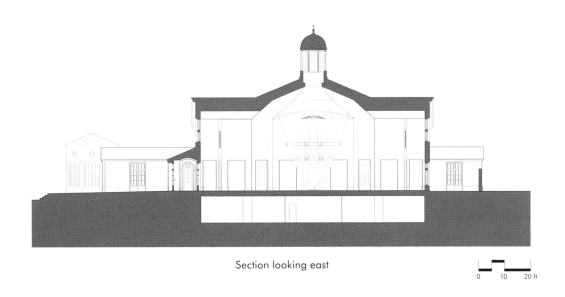

Section looking east

0   10   20 ft

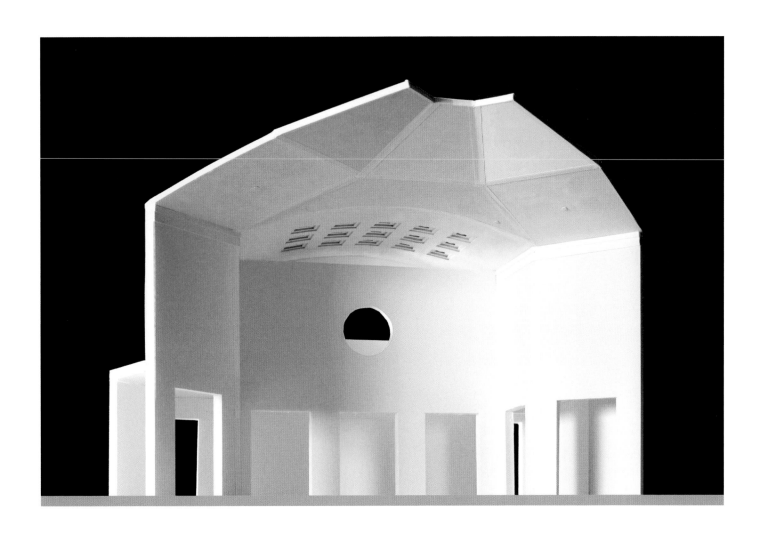

Residences on Zero Island

Tianjin, China
2011–
Project Partners:
Grant F. Marani
Paul L. Whalen

Top: Villa 3.

Bottom: Villa 2.

An island of freestanding villas and townhouses, connected to the mainland by two bridges, is inspired by Tianjin's rich heritage of late nineteenth- and early twentieth-century Western-influenced residential architecture. An elliptical central green forms the development's heart, while smaller parks set along radial roads aerate the plan. A continuous public path along the waterfront leads to a marina at the north end of the island and a clubhouse to the south.

Master plan

0   25   50 m

Museum of the American Revolution

Philadelphia, Pennsylvania
2011–2016
Project Partners:
Alexander P. Lamis
Kevin M. Smith

Anchoring the eastern end of Independence National Historical Park at the corner of Chestnut and Third Streets, the Museum of the American Revolution will introduce visitors to the themes of the War of Independence. The design reflects the Colonial and early Republican architecture that characterizes its setting. A broad plaza leads to an entrance pavilion set against a stone tympanum surmounted by an open loggia. Recessed brick arches with apsidal stone niches will articulate the mass of galleries above a museum shop and a café, helping to enliven Third Street. A grand elliptical stair set in a skylit interior court will take visitors up to the galleries and a theater dedicated to the exhibition of George Washington's marquee tent, one of the museum's most dramatic holdings.

Second floor plan

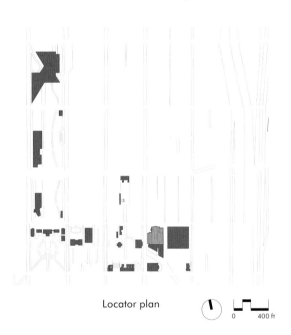

Locator plan

0   400 ft

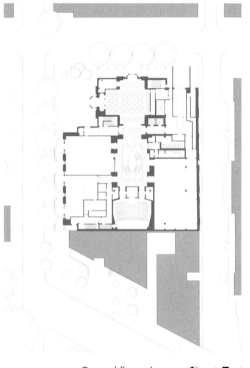

Ground floor plan

0   16 32 ft

Top: View looking southeast from Chestnut and Third Streets.

Left bottom: View looking northeast along Third Street.

Right bottom: View looking east to entry plaza.

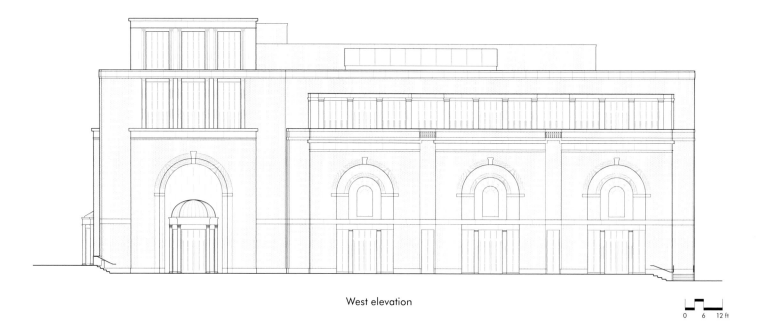

West elevation

0   6   12 ft

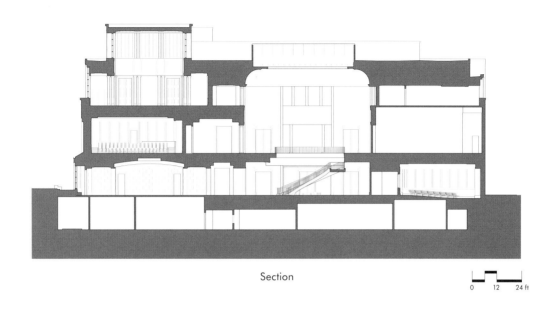

Section

Damrak 70

Amsterdam, The Netherlands
2011–
Project Partners:
Paul L. Whalen
Daniel Lobitz

Sited on an important civic plaza in the center of Amsterdam, opposite H.P. Berlage's Beurs (1903), our design reinterprets Amsterdam's traditional palette of limestone and brick to present a contemporary expression that is in harmony with the building's smaller-scale neighbors. Syncopated fenestration and angled bays respond to the building's visibility across the broad plaza as well as the very acute angles from which the building will be approached along nearby narrow streets. Double-height shopfronts and an open-air shop-lined passage weave the building into the lively pedestrian experience of Amsterdam's fine-grained urban fabric.

Ground floor plan

0   5   10 m

Site plan

0   25   50 m

Left: Passage.

Right top: Passage
entry at Damrak.

Right bottom:
Passage entry from
Nieuwendijk.

Dalian AVIC
International Square

Dalian, China
2011–2015 (Phase I)
Project Partners:
Grant F. Marani
Paul L. Whalen
Michael D. Jones

Covering four city blocks on a five-hectare site, this 352,000-square-meter mixed-use city-within-a-city comprises four residential towers each on two blocks, a high-rise office and apartment tower on the third block, and a mid-rise apartment building and a mid-rise office building on the fourth block. The new neighborhood will become a new hub of pedestrian activity for the Zhongshan financial district, with garden courtyards between the residential towers and plazas lined with shopfronts between the office buildings.

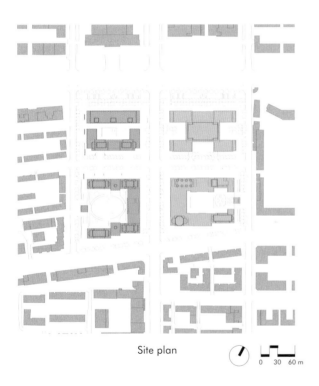

Site plan

0   30   60 m

Below: Aerial view
looking southwest.

Top left: Preserving the street grid.

Top right: Defining gardens and courtyards.

Bottom left: Perimeter buildings relating to low-rise neighbors.

Bottom right: Towers set back from peripheral streets.

Right: View looking east from courtyard fountain.

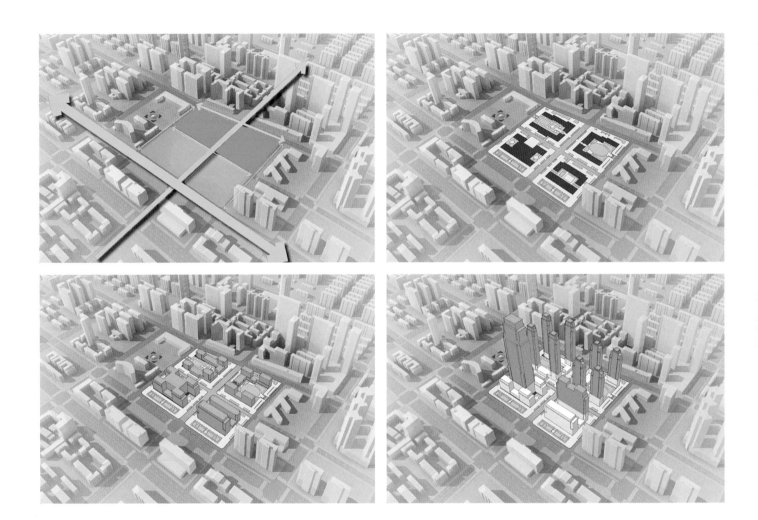

Top: Office building
entry.

Bottom: Residential
building entry.

Below: Residential
tower crowns.

Right: Office tower.

Top: Construction
view looking
southeast.

Bottom: Construction
view of office entry.

Top: Construction
view looking
southwest.

Bottom: Construction
view of retail.

Barkli Residence

Moscow, Russia
2012–2016
Project Partner:
Kevin M. Smith

Right: View looking
west.

Inspired by Moscow's tradition of towers with elaborate silhouettes, Barkli Residence will provide 154 apartments. Two towers define a motor court and public garden set atop a shop-lined podium that helps weave the composition into the streetscape. Pilasters, cornices, balconies, bay windows, and loggias articulate the granite-trimmed, cast stone-clad buildings as they rise through a series of setbacks to culminate in penthouses.

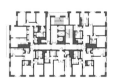

Typical floor plan

Locator plan

0 30 60 m

Ground floor plan

0 5 10 m

Schwarzman College

Tsinghua University
Beijing, China
2012–2016
Project Partners:
Graham S. Wyatt
Melissa DelVecchio

Much like the program in global leadership and international relations it will house, Schwarzman College is designed to harmonize Eastern and Western principles. The organization of the building around two courtyards—one interior to the building and one facing the street—recalls both traditional Oxford and Cambridge colleges and the courtyard houses of China. A double-height forum, serving as an informal social space as well as a venue for lectures and large gatherings, welcomes visitors and residents alike, with library and dining hall wings to either side. Classrooms and a conference center surround a sunken interior garden court, with an auditorium located below. Two hundred scholars will live in single rooms organized in groups of eight sharing a common lounge, an arrangement intended to foster close relationships. Clad in the gray brick characteristic of Beijing, accented with stone and wood details, large windows, and traditional tile roofs, the design seeks to reflect the College's spirit of cultural collaboration.

Site plan

0   25   50 m

Below: Aerial view
looking northwest.

Below: East-west
section perspective.

Right top: View
looking southwest.

Right bottom: Sunken
courtyard.

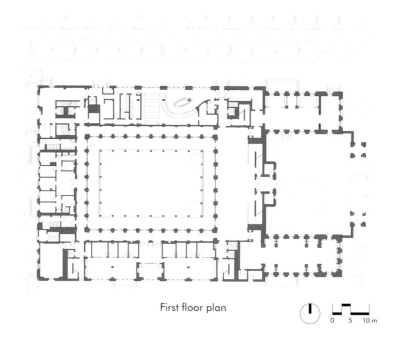

First floor plan

0   5   10 m

Top: Forum
configured as lounge.

Bottom: Forum
configured for special
events.

Hangyue Liangjiang Town Center

Chongqing, China
2012–
Project Partners:
Grant F. Marani
Paul L. Whalen
Michael D. Jones

Top: South courtyard at retail village.

Middle: Entry plaza.

Bottom: North courtyard at retail village.

This mountaintop resort on the outskirts of Chongqing consists of a retail village, now under construction, and a hotel and conference center expected to start construction in 2015. Visitors arrive at a landscaped plaza and ascend a grand stair that climbs though a gateway arch to a series of pedestrian squares and shopping terraces with views to the valley below. Above the retail village, an oval lawn sized for large receptions will serve a wedding chapel conceived as a garden pavilion; to the north is a lookout tower, to the south, an amphitheater. The entry drive runs along the west side of the ridge to the hotel that overlooks the dramatic landscape where, in subsequent phases, villas will dot the hillside.

Master plan

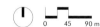

0   45   90 m

Heavener Hall

Heavener College of Business
Warrington College of
Business Administration
University of Florida
Gainesville, Florida
2012–2014
Project Partners:
Graham S. Wyatt
Melissa DelVecchio

Top: Construction
view looking west.

Bottom: Center for
Student Achievement.

Reflecting the University's distinctive Collegiate Gothic expression of Gainesville red brick, clay roof tile, and limestone and white-painted wood detailing developed by William Augustus Edwards in the 1920s, Heavener Hall is sited on a highly visible site where the historic campus meets the city of Gainesville. The L-shaped building surrounds a new, landscaped courtyard and frames a pedestrian entrance to the College of Business precinct from University Avenue. On the ground floor, a student commons, multipurpose room, and café all open to outdoor terraces. Seven classrooms, a student lounge, and breakout rooms are located on the second floor; faculty and staff offices are located on the third floor.

Campus plan   0 64 128 ft

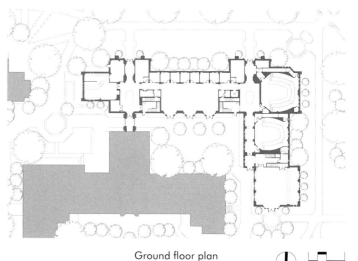

Ground floor plan   0 20 40 ft

Deluxe Bay

Jindong New District
Jinhua, Zhejiang, China
2012–
Project Partners:
Grant F. Marani
Paul L. Whalen

Top: South plaza.

Middle: Courtyard.

Bottom: Aerial rendering.

Three-story buildings accommodating shops and offices line a street punctuated by a variety of courtyards that weave the complex into an existing urban neighborhood. To the south, a civic-scaled plaza steps down to address the pavilions of the Jinhua Architecture Park on the lakefront. To the north, a second phase of development now under construction will introduce a large central square connecting to smaller-scale sidestreets, two highrise apartment buildings, and two highrise office buildings set atop retail and a cinema. The vocabulary of stone accented with metal and wood detailing and tile roofs is a cosmopolitan take on local architectural traditions.

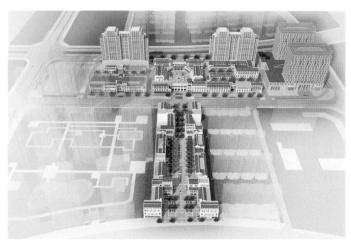

Northwestern
Lake Forest Hospital

Lake Forest, Illinois
Competition, 2012
Project Partner:
Graham S. Wyatt
Augusta Barone
Kevin M. Smith

Top: Gallery.

Bottom: Section.

To reduce this new hospital's apparent size, our plan organized four-story patient care pavilions along a crescent anchored by a central winter garden serving as a principal lobby and opening to reconstructed prairie landscape beyond. A triple-height gallery accommodating comfortably furnished waiting areas connected the pavilions and intervening gardens.

Rustic Wisconsin limestone trimmed with smooth-cut Indiana limestone complements residential Lake Forest, while the winter garden and glassy galleries carry forward the modern aesthetic of Northwestern Medical Center's downtown Chicago campus.

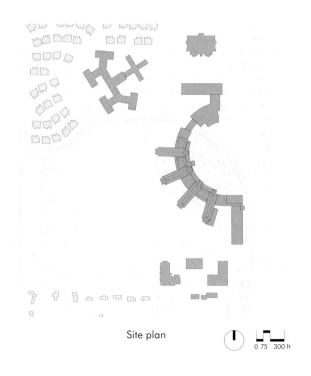

Site plan

0 75 300 ft

1601 Vine Street

Philadelphia, Pennsylvania
2012–
Project Partners:
Paul L. Whalen
Sargent C. Gardiner

Filling an important gap in Philadelphia's urban
fabric, a residential tower and a meetinghouse for the
Church of Jesus Christ of Latter-day Saints will be tied
together by their common inspiration in Philadelphia's
strong tradition of brick architecture. While the point
of reference for the meetinghouse is Colonial-era red-
brick Georgian, for the tower it is the buff-brick and
stone typical of many of the city's apartment buildings
of the 1920s and 30s, with symmetrical facades enliv-
ened by setbacks, balconies, terraces, and groupings
of windows traced in stone trim, rising to a sculpted
skyline profile.

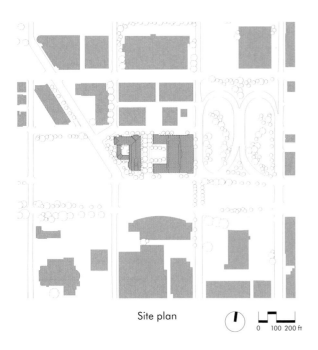

Site plan

0   100 200 ft

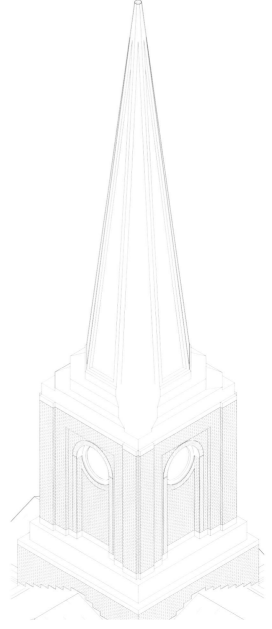

Steeple axonometric

Top: View looking northeast from Logan Square.

Bottom left: Aerial view looking northeast.

Bottom right: View looking west along Vine Street.

New York Residences

Ak Bulak
Astana, Kazakhstan
2013–
Partner:
Grant F. Marani

Inspired by Riverside Park and its bounding wall of apartment houses, Ak Bulak, bordering the Esil River, will group four residential towers at the north end of the site around a clubhouse that will open to a broad plaza overlooking a marina and connecting to a meandering riverwalk in its first phase. Later phases will thread through formal and informal gardens, leading to a fifth tower that will punctuate the southern end of the composition. Covered walkways between the residential buildings are a response to Astana's extreme winters.

Top: Park.

Bottom: View of clubhouse from promenade.

Top: View looking west from marina.

Bottom: View looking southwest along Orynbor Street.

Additional Projects

Apartment on Fifth Avenue
New York, New York, 2004–2006
Project Partner: Seifter

A 1960s open-plan apartment is reorganized with
intimately-scaled formal rooms opening from an
elliptical foyer. To camouflage ribbon windows, an inner
liner of vertically-proportioned openings frames views
to Central Park. Louis XVI and Directoire details,
acknowledging our client's preference for all things
French, provide a sense of height.

Las Olas
Coral Isles, Fort Lauderdale, Florida, 2006–2014
Project Partner: Seifter

A sinuous plan orients the principal rooms of this
Mediterranean Revival house to waterfront views;
galleries buffer the living spaces from nearby neighbors.

Apartment at 15 Central Park West
New York, New York, 2007–2010
Project Partners: Seifter, Lamis

In a pied-à-terre designed for business entertaining and
family gatherings, twentieth-century French furniture
and new classical modern pieces designed by our office
give pride of place to the views and to the owners'
museum-quality art collection.

Harmony Cove
Trelawny, Jamaica, Project, 2007–2008
Project Partners: Gardiner, Lobitz, Whalen

A waterfront resort on a 2,400-acre site 30 minutes east
of Montego Bay wraps a yacht harbor with hotels, shops,
villas, and music venues fronting stone-paved plazas and
intimate streets.

Brooklyn Law School Lobby
Brooklyn Law School
Brooklyn, New York, 2008–2009
Project Partner: Whalen

Fifteen years after the completion of our Brooklyn Law
School tower, we returned to improve the lobby of the
School's 1968 building.

424

Apartment at 820 Park Avenue
New York, New York, 2008–2012
Project Partner: Seifter

A relaxed classical vocabulary lends a youthful yet dignified informality to this full-floor apartment.

 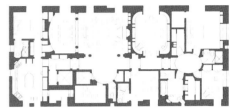

The Estates at Keswick Hall
Keswick, Virginia, Project, 2009
Project Partners: Lobitz, Correll, Marani, Seifter

Asked to develop ideas for lots surrounding a historic mansion in the rolling hills east of Charlottesville, we proposed five stylistic interpretations of traditional country villas: Palladian, Mediterranean, Italianate, Georgian, and Regency.

Mixed-Use Development
Boulogne-Billancourt, France, Competition, 2009
Project Partners: McDermott, Smith, Wyatt

To support a sustainable live/work community, we proposed an office building with vertical fritted-glass sunshades, residential buildings with fixed and sliding glass-and-metal panels, and landscaped courtyards.

U.S. Courthouse
Billings, Montana, Competition, 2009
Project Partner: Marani

Organized on classical principles to express the dignity of the American judicial system, our proposal placed court sets to either side of a central atrium offering views to the historic downtown and to nearby dramatic sandstone outcroppings known as the Rims.

Redlich Hall
The Hotchkiss School
Lakeville, Connecticut, 2009–
Project Partners: Wyatt, Gumberich

Replacing an outworn dormitory from the 1890s, Redlich Hall continues our strategy of bookending a red-brick central mass with gambrel-roofed wings accommodating faculty apartments and porches to complete the residential quadrangle established by Flinn and Edelman Halls (2007).

425

College of Law
University of Illinois at Urbana-Champaign
Urbana, Illinois, Project, 2009–2010
Project Partners: Lamis, Lobitz

Complementing the predominant Charles Platt-designed Georgian architecture of the campus, an H-shaped building embraces a glass-enclosed commons and an open courtyard. A freestanding "courthouse," accommodating an auditorium and a mock courtroom, occupies a critical position at the head of a cross-campus mall.

Colin Powell School for Civic and Global Leadership
CUNY/City College of New York
New York, New York, Competition, 2010
Project Partners: Wyatt, Barone

Our proposal interprets the schist facades and terra-cotta trim of George B. Post's original buildings for City College (1903-1907) at the larger scale of its late-twentieth-century Modernist neighbors.

Seorak Sorano
Hanwha Seorak Resort, Kangwondo, Korea, Project, 2010–2012
Project Partners: Wyatt, Smith

The romantically-massed centerpiece of our 2008 master plan for the Seorak resort complements the Mediterranean vocabulary of two renovated existing hotels and overlooks, in the manner of a Tuscan hill town, a surrounding "village" of golf villas.

Apartment at 15 Central Park West
New York, New York, 2010–2012
Project Partner: Seifter

The neutral palette of this two-bedroom pied-à-terre complements the owners' mid-century American and European furniture and provides an understated backdrop to their collection of contemporary art.

Capital City
Noida, Uttar Pradesh, India, 2010–
Project Partners: Whalen, Gardiner

On an important highway approach to Noida, a satellite of New Delhi, office buildings wrap a retail mall, the roof of which is developed as a landscaped forecourt for the offices.

Becker Business Building
Barney Barnett School of Business
Florida Southern College, 2010–2015
Project Partner: Lamis

Anchoring the southeast corner of campus, the Becker Building continues the Frank Lloyd Wright-inspired palette of precast panels, stucco, and painted metalwork used for our three previous buildings at the College. Deep overhangs and legacy oaks will shade a glass curtainwall facing Lake Hollingsworth.

Residences on Mount Nicholson Road
Hong Kong, 2010–2015
Project Partner: Marani

Asked to contribute to a residential enclave set on a heavily-wooded peninsular ridge with spectacular views overlooking Hong Kong Central, we reworked the streetscape and entry sequence, redesigned the facades of two residential towers, designed two out of 19 villas, and fitted out a model penthouse and two villas.

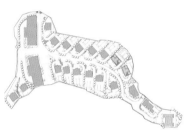

House at West Chop
Vineyard Haven, Martha's Vineyard, Massachusetts, 2011–2015
Project Partner: Brewer

Set on Main Street among historic houses, this shingled cottage is organized to take advantage of views to Vineyard Sound, the Atlantic Ocean, and its own private garden. Picturesque gables and dormers, classical eaves, painted wood shutters, window boxes, and a flower-covered trellis carry forward the great tradition of Martha's Vineyard summer retreats.

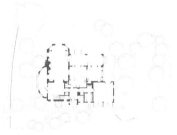

Student Residences on Lancaster Avenue
Villanova University
Villanova, Pennsylvania, 2011–
Project Partners: Wyatt, Smith

Linked by arched passageways, stone-clad Collegiate Gothic residential quadrangles will face alternately north to Lancaster Avenue and Villanova's historic campus core and south to a light-rail stop and the university's South Campus. Ground-level retail and a new fitness center along Lancaster Avenue will buffer the student residences from the busy street.

Performance Arts Center
Villanova University
Villanova, Pennsylvania, 2012–
Project Partners: Wyatt, Smith

Continuing our interpretation of Villanova's Collegiate Gothic character developed for the residences halls, but with a more open expression appropriate to a public arts venue, our design addresses Lancaster Avenue with the welcoming curve of its lobby wrapping the windowless box of the theater.

Residences on Barker Road
Hong Kong, Project, 2011
Project Partner: Marani

To take advantage of unobstructed harbor views from a steeply-sloping site, our design for a family compound on Victoria Peak set three private villas on a large lawn cantilevered above a podium.

900 16th Street, NW
Washington, DC, 2011–2015
Project Partner: Wyatt

A limestone and glass nine-story office building incorporates a distinctly identifiable entrance to the Third Church of Christ, Scientist, that is incorporated within.

Residences on Dun Hua South Road
Taipei, Taiwan, Project, 2011–2012
Project Partners: Marani, Whalen, Gardiner

A 46-story limestone residential tower was intended to offer 58 large simplex and duplex apartments, with a triplex penthouse at the crown.

Residence
Mountain Lake, Florida, 2011–2014
Project Partner: Seifter

A renovation of a 1929 house by architect Franklin W. Abbott restores details and finishes that had been lost over time. A new enclosure for the pool, anchored by an open-loggia poolhouse, continues the narrative.

Residence in Golf Links
New Delhi, India, 2011–
Project Partners: Seifter, Whalen

Overlooking a park, and surrounded by its own garden rooms, this villa, now under construction, complements the Anglo-Indian classicism of Sir Edwin Lutyens.

31 Conduit Road
Hong Kong, 2011–
Project Partners: Marani, Whalen, Gardiner

Limestone and granite facades, incorporating vegetated panels, bronze metalwork, and decorative lattice screens, help distinguish the base of this residential tower from its glass curtainwall neighbors. Where the building steps back at the fifth level, a pool deck and garden face the verdant hillside that rises to Victoria Peak. Above, the building's fenestration expresses the variety of floor-through residences within.

Arris
1331 4th Street, SE, The Yards
Washington, DC, 2012–2015
Project Partners: Whalen, Gardiner

Complementing industrial buildings now converted for residential and commercial uses at what was until recently an annex to the Washington Navy Yard, this residential building activates a rapidly changing neighborhood with shops on three sides. Above a brick base, an undulating crystalline superstructure takes advantage of Anacostia River views.

15 LEGO Park West
Model for the National Building Museum's Exhibit "LEGO Architecture: Towering Ambition," 2012

Created for the National Building Museum's exhibition "LEGO Architecture: Towering Ambition," this 1/16"-scale model affirms 15 Central Park West's status as one of the world's most recognized residential buildings.

Admissions Building
Elon University
Elon, North Carolina, 2012–2015
Project Partners: Wyatt, Smith

A Georgian composition, complete with a central rotunda topped with a cupola and framed by wings anchored by open loggias, will introduce visitors to Elon's historic campus and serve as the starting point for prospective student tours. The building's south facade defines a new quadrangle opening towards the University's main library.

School of Communications
Elon University
Elon, North Carolina, 2012–
Project Partners: Wyatt, Smith

A transparent commons pavilion, intended to serve as an event space, will link our building to the School of Communications' existing McEwen Building. Window walls will offer passersby views into the School's television studio; the long north facade will enclose Elon's oak-canopied graduation quadrangle.

House in Edgartown
Martha's Vineyard, Massachusetts, Project, 2012
Project Partner: Brewer

A modest existing vernacular clapboard house in Edgartown's historic center is tripled in size.

Gatton College of Business and Economics
University of Kentucky, Lexington, Kentucky, 2012–2016
Project Partners: Wyatt, Smith

Unifying a 1960s building and a 1990s addition, this 65,000-square-foot classroom wing will wrap a light-flooded atrium. Limestone and brick facades continue the campus palette, while expansive window walls showcase Gatton's new classrooms to the outside world.

Shepherd University Master Plan
Shepherdstown, West Virginia, 2012
Project Partners: Wyatt, Barone

Our plan proposes new buildings and a network of pedestrian-friendly paths to strengthen connections between two lobes of Shepherd's existing campus and—importantly—the university's relationship to the Potomac River.

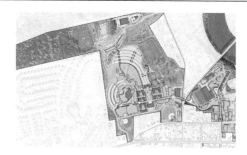

Correll Hall
Terry College of Business, University of Georgia
Athens, Georgia, 2012–2015
Project Partners: Wyatt, Smith

On the northern tier of a sloping site adjacent to the University's historic core, the red-brick Correll Hall—the first phase of a three-phase Business Learning Community—incorporates Greek Revival motifs characteristic of the Athens campus.

Three Otter Farm
Edgartown, Martha's Vineyard, Massachusetts, 2012–
Project Partner: Seifter

A shingled farmhouse connects to the landscape with sweeping curves that orient the principal rooms and porches to light and to views of woodland, meadows, and a tidal pond on the south shore of Martha's Vineyard.

Pezet I
San Isidro, Lima, Peru, 2012–2015
Project Partners: Whalen, Jones

This 22-story limestone residential tower takes advantage of views over the Lima Golf Club. Lima's temperate climate encourages easy flow between the interiors and generously-sized open loggias.

College of Business Administration
University of Nebraska
Lincoln, Nebraska, 2012–
Project Partners: Wyatt, DelVecchio

Masonry-clad wings housing faculty offices and classrooms flank a four-story atrium that runs the full length of the building; an iconic glass-clad cube on axis with Memorial Stadium will raise the visibility of the college on all-important football weekends.

Additions to the International Tennis Hall of Fame
Newport, Rhode Island, 2013–
Project Partner: Brewer

McKim, Mead & White's Newport Casino (1880), among the most influential early examples of the Shingle Style, has served as home of the Tennis Hall of Fame since 1954. Our work includes reorganizing the campus to accommodate improved indoor and outdoor courts and a new tennis center that addresses Memorial Boulevard in the manner of the original building.

Blossom Plaza
Santa Monica, California, Competition, 2013
Project Partners: Whalen, Gardiner

To promote ever-changing public programming—art festivals, farmers' markets, movie nights—at the intersection of 4th Street and Arizona Avenue, we proposed an adaptable civic space extending into the lower floors of an office building, designed as a small-business incubator, and apartment blocks intended for artists.

Courier Square
Charleston, South Carolina, 2013–
Project Partner: Brewer

On a full-block site north of Charleston's traditional downtown, two contrasting buildings—a stone and stucco-clad six-story office building inspired by historic commercial development and an eight-story red-brick residential block, designed to evoke the spirit of the neighborhood's industrial lofts—will wrap parking topped by a swimming pool deck.

House at Jackstay Court
Kiawah Island, South Carolina, 2013–
Project Partner: Brewer

A low-slung shingled cottage faces the ocean beach and the ocean with broad porches and a second-floor balcony nestled between twin gambrels.

Hoover Dining Hall
DePauw University
Greencastle, Indiana, 2013-2016
Project Partners: Wyatt, Gumberich

Helping to revitalize the center of campus, this restrained red-brick Georgian building will accommodate 700 diners. Improvements to the adjacent Hubbard Center for Student Engagement will follow in a future phase.

Angelo, Gordon & Co.
New York, New York, 2013–2015
Project Partners: Correll, Lamis

Three floors of offices for an investment firm are dramatically linked by interior stairs. A sleek aesthetic is counterpointed by mid-twentieth-century furniture and a collection of important Modern and contemporary art.

Lake House
Lakeside, Michigan, 2013–
Project Partner: Correll

The simple gabled mass of this shingled guest house embraces deep porches and a terrace with views to Lake Michigan.

House on Eugenia Avenue
Kiawah Island, South Carolina, 2013–
Project Partner: Brewer

Set atop the dune, this double-gabled shingled house will address the ocean with a deep porch wrapping the principal rooms.

Project Credits

Project Credits

The Clarendon / One Back Bay
Boston, Massachusetts

Partners: Michael D. Jones, Paul L. Whalen. Senior Associate: Michael D. Jones. Associates: Bina Bhattacharyya. Project Manager: Tad Roemer. Team: Gaylin M. Bowie, Dax Gardiner, Annie Mennes, Adele Lim. Interior Design Associates: Ken Stuckenschneider. Interior Design Assistants: Hyung Kee Lee, Alys Stephens Protzman. Associate Architects: CBT Architects, Ismael Leyva Architects. Landscape Architect: Copley Wolff Design Group.

Robert A.M. Stern: Buildings and Projects 2004–2009 (New York: The Monacelli Press, 2009), 334–37.
Curtis Kemeny, "Are Lofts Still Hip?" *Urban Land,* March 2009, 113–14, 116.
Meghan Agnew, "Condo Library Provides a Study in Style and Substance," *The Boston Globe,* February 11, 2010.
Rachel Levitt, "Battle of the Condo Buildings," *Boston,* February 2010, 30.
John T. O'Connor, "So You're Thinking of Living at ...The Clarendon," *Esplanade,* March/April 2010, 58–60.
Alison Mapplethorpe, "Urban Eden," *Design New England,* September/October 2010, 66, 68, 70.
"Back Bay Luxury Project Beats the Odds, Hits 50% Sold," *Boston Herald,* March 7, 2011.
Daniel Geiger, "The Related Cos. Reaches Deeper Into Boston," *Crain's New York Business,* April 8, 2013.
Charlie Abrahams, "The Clarendon in Boston's Back Bay Is 100% Sold Out," *Boston Herald,* August 15, 2013.
"Related Beal Sells Out the Clarendon With Final Penthouse Sold for $6.2 Million," *New England Real Estate Journal,* September 6, 2011.
"Rendered in Glass and Brick," *Architecture + Design,* August 2013, 102–6.

Arthur and Janet Ross Children's Addition
East Hampton Library, East Hampton, New York

Partner: Randy M. Correll. Project Managers: Hannah Cho, Christian N. Dickson. Team: Brent Locey. Interior Design (Children's Room): Lee H. Skolnick Architecture + Design Partnership.

Robert A.M. Stern: Buildings and Projects 1993–1998 (New York: The Monacelli Press, 1998), 170–73.
Carissa Katz, "Library Scales Back New Wing Plan," *The East Hampton Star,* August 5, 2004.
Carissa Katz, "Ready to Roll Out Children's Wing," *The East Hampton Star,* December 21, 2006, A:1, 3.
"A First Look at Library's Addition," *The East Hampton Star,* February 21, 2008, A:6.
Carissa Katz, "Homework to Do on Children's Wing," *The East Hampton Star,* February 28, 2008, A:1, 3.
Carissa Katz, "On Library Size, Legal Quandary Dogs Village," *The East Hampton Star,* May 1, 2008, A:4.
Amanda Gordon, "Partying in Honor of a Glamorous Locale's Local Library," *The New York Sun,* August 11, 2008, 2.
"East Hampton's War Against the Library," *The East Hampton Star,* January 1, 2009, B:1.
Carissa Katz, "Children's Wing Expansion Logjam," *The East Hampton Star,* July 2, 2009, A:1, 5.
Selim Algar, "The Book Shnooks on E. End," *New York Post,* August 1, 2009, 3.
Carissa Katz, "Public Speaks Volumes on Library," *The East Hampton Star,* September 17, 2009, A:1, 4.
Leigh Goodstein, "Library Talks Collapse," *The East Hampton Star,* July 15, 2010, A:1, 5.
Carissa Katz, "Library Expansion Gets Straw Poll Saturday," *The East Hampton Star,* August 12, 2010, A:3.
Erin Geismar, "Voters Overwhelmingly Support East Hampton Library Expansion Plans," *27 East,* August 17, 2010.
Ian Ratner, "Plot Twist for East Hampton Library Expansion," *Curbed,* August 17, 2010.
Sara Polsky, "East Hampton Wants Its Robert A.M. Stern Library," *Curbed,* August 20, 2010.
Bridget LeRoy and Carissa Katz, "Children's Wing Wins Approval," *The East Hampton Star,* May 26, 2011, A:1, 4.
Bridget LeRoy, "Library Approval Is Official," *The East Hampton Star,* June 30, 2011, A:4.
Bridget LeRoy, "Library Buoyed by Gift: Alec Baldwin Donates $250,000 for Children's Wing," *The East Hampton Star,* November 11, 2011, A:1, 2.
Stephen J, Kotz, "East Hampton Library Breaks Ground—Finally," *27 East,* April 16, 2012.
Christopher Walsh, "Baldwin Donates a Cool Mil," *The East Hampton Star,* November 14, 2013, A:1, 3.
Christopher Walsh, "Children's Wing Done by Late Spring?" *The East Hampton Star,* March 6, 2014, A:3.
Christopher Walsh, "Children's Wing Is Welcomed," *The East Hampton Star,* June 26, 2014, A:1, 3.
Will James, "Check It Out! The East Hampton Library Children's Wing Opens at Last," *Newsday LI Life,* G:1, 4–7.

10 Rittenhouse Square
Philadelphia, Pennsylvania

Partners: Graham S. Wyatt. Associate: Breen Mahony. Team: Daniel Arbelaez, Gregory Christopher, Laura Dunne, Kasumi Hara, Leonid Khanin, Miguel Lasala, Don Lee, Katherine LoBalbo, Ryan Rodenberg, Lindsay Weiss. Interior Design Associate: Ken Stuckenschneider. Interior Design Assistants: Khara Nemitz. Landscape Design Senior Associate: Michael Weber. Landscape Design Project Manager: Ashley Christopher. Landscape Design Assistant: Mark Rodriguez. Associate Architects: Ismael Leyva Architects, Polatnick Zacharjasz Architects.

Robert A.M. Stern: Buildings and Projects 2004–2009 (New York: The Monacelli Press, 2009), 346–47.
Inga Saffron, "Rittenhouse Square's Traditionalist Pretender," *The Philadelphia Inquirer,* January 22, 2010, E:1, 3.
Alan J. Heavens, "Pension Fund Takes Over Luxury Condos," *The Philadelphia Inquirer,* July 20, 2010, A:1, 4.
Alan J. Heavens, "Senior Lender for Condo Files for Foreclosure," *The Philadelphia Inquirer,* September 22, 2010.
Robbie Whelan, "Another Dream Goes Bust," *The Wall Street Journal,* November 17, 2010, C:10.
Maura Webber Sadovi, "Real Estate Wars Go On," *The Wall Street Journal,* January 26, 2011, C:6.
Kevin McMahon, "Facadism at Rittenhouse," *Prospectus* (a publication of the University of Pennsylvania's Graduate Program in Historic Preservation), Vol. 3 (2011), 48–53.
Alyssa Abkowitz, "Comcast CEO Roberts Buys High in Philly," *The Wall Street Journal,* October 19, 2012, M:2.

East Academic Building
Webster University, Webster Groves, Missouri

Partners: Kevin M. Smith, Graham S. Wyatt. Associate: Sue Jin Sung. Team: Daniel Arbelaez, Leo Khanin, Eric Silinsh, Michael Tabacinic, Saul Uranovsky Interior Design Associates: Hyung Kee Lee, Ken Stuckenschneider. Associate Architect: Mackey Mitchell Associates.

Robert A.M. Stern: Buildings and Projects 2004–2009 (New York: The Monacelli Press, 2009), 585.

Matthew Hibbard, "Webster Unveils $29 Million Business School Building," *St. Louis Business Journal*, March 28, 2012.

Wasserstein Hall, Caspersen Student Center, and Clinical Wing
Harvard Law School, Cambridge, Massachusetts

Project Partners: Melissa DelVecchio, Alexander P. Lamis, Kevin M. Smith, Graham S. Wyatt. Senior Associates: Kurt Glauber, Jennifer L. Stone. Associates: Sophia Cha, George de Brigard, Wing Yee Ng Fung-Fortugno, Don Johnson, Christopher LaSala, Oliver Pelle, Sue Jin Sung, Kim Yap. Team: Taytana Albinder, Thomas Brady, Andrew Donaldson, Lorenzo Galati, Dennis George, Natalie Goldberg, Milton Hernandez, William Holloway, Jennifer Lee, William Perez, Kaveri Singh, Jennifer Smith, Brian Taylor. Interior Design Associate: Shannon Ratcliff. Interior Design Assistants: Tina Hu, Crystal Palleschi, Aruni Weerasinghe. Model Builder: Victor Marcelino. Landscape Architect: Halvorson Design Partnership.

Robert A.M. Stern: Buildings and Projects 2004–2009 (New York: The Monacelli Press, 2009), 410–11.
Robert M. Brandon and Arthur Spruch, "Campus Improvement Begins With Planning," *Architectural Products*, April 2009, 12.
Robert A.M. Stern: On Campus (New York: The Monacelli Press, 2010), 252–59, 282–85.
Martha Minow, "Raise High the Roof Beam," *Harvard Law Bulletin*, Winter 2010, 1.
"Ambitions Realized," *Harvard Magazine*, May/June 2011.
Jonathan Shaw, "Building—and Buying—a Campus," *Harvard Magazine*, September/October 2011.
Robert Campbell, "Tradition Embodied at Harvard," *The Boston Globe*, December 11, 2011, N:5.
"Moving In," *Harvard Law Today*, January 2012, 8.
Colleen Walsh, "In the Spirit of the Law," *Harvard Gazette*, April 19, 2012.
Colleen Walsh, "Law School Dedicates New Building," *Harvard Gazette*, April 23, 2012.
Martha Minow, "Environment and Community," *Harvard Law Bulletin*, Summer 2012, 2.
"The Way We Live Now: A Day in the Life," *Harvard Law Bulletin*, Summer 2012, 34–38.
Mavis Linneman, "Setting a Firm Foundation for Harvard Law," *Architectural Products*, November 2012, 86.

Richard T. Farmer School of Business
Miami University, Oxford, Ohio

Partners: Preston J. Gumberich, Graham S. Wyatt. Senior Associate: Jeffery Povero. Associate: George Punnoose. Project Manager: Sean Foley. Team: Daniel Arbalaez, Afzal Hossain, Jill Lagowski, Meredith Micale, Michael Ryan, Yok Saowasang, Jeremy Shannon, Michael Tabacinic, Rob Teeters. Interior Design Associate: Shannon Ratcliff. Interior Design Assistants: Michelle Everett, Taylor Stein. Model Builders: David Abecassis, Bruce Lindsay. Associate Architect: Moody Nolan. Landscape Architect: James Burkart Associates.

Robert A.M. Stern: Buildings and Projects 2004–2009 (New York: The Monacelli Press, 2009), 412–13.
Robert A.M. Stern: On Campus (New York: The Monacelli Press, 2010), 402–13.
Edwin Heathcote, "Outside the Box: New Architecture for Business Schools," *Financial Times*, January 31, 2011.
Lynne Lavelle, "Open for Business," *Traditional Building*, October 2011, 18–21.
Alison Damast, "A New Twist in B-School Recruiting," *Bloomberg Businessweek*, April 3, 2012.

One Museum Mile
1280 Fifth Avenue, New York, New York

Partners: Daniel Lobitz, Paul L. Whalen. Associates: Gaylin M. Bowie, Michael Soriano. Project Architect: Chen-Huan Liao. Team: Lina Ayala, Ravi D'Cruz, Jorge Fontan, Wing Yee Ng Fung-Fortugno, Kyung Sook Gemma Kim, Aileen Park, Ellen Willis. Interior Design Associate: John Boyland. Interior Design Assistant: Mitra Moshari. Associate Architect: SLCE Architects, G Tects.

Robert A.M. Stern: Buildings and Projects 2004–2009 (New York: The Monacelli Press, 2009), 422–25.
C.J. Hughes, "At the Intersection of Art and Nature," *The New York Times*, November 29, 2009, Real Estate: 7.
Norval White and Elliott Wilensky, *AIA Guide to New York City*, fifth edition (Oxford University Press, 2010), 523.
Sara Polsky, "1280 Fifth's Facade Pattern Is Here, Sales Office Coming This Spring," *Curbed*, February 1, 2010.
Joey Arak, "What to Expect Inside Robert A.M. Stern's 1280 Fifth," *Curbed*, May 21, 2010.
Josephine Minutillo, "Stern's Museum for African Art Set to Open in 2011," *Architectural Record*, May 19, 2010.
Sharon McHugh, "New Address for NYC's Museum Mile," *World Architecture News*, May 24, 2010.
Katherine Dykstra, "Rounding Out Museum Mile: African Art Venue Heads to 1280 Fifth Avenue, and Brings Along a Condo," *The Real Deal*, May 2010, 46.
Sara Polsky, "Robert A.M. Stern's 1280 Fifth Avenue Hits the Market," *Curbed*, June 10, 2010.
Kate Taylor, "Pulling Museum Mile Uptown," *The New York Times*, June 20, 2010, Arts & Leisure: 1, 23.
Sabrina Chapman, "A New Kid on the Block at 1280 Fifth Avenue," *Haute Living*, July 15, 2010.
Fred A. Bernstein, "Pushing the Boundary of Luxe," *The New York Times*, July 25, 2010, Real Estate: 1, 8.
Kate Taylor, "African Art Museum Again Delays Opening of Site on Fifth Avenue," *The New York Times*, September 4, 2010, C:3.
Sara Polsky, "Robert A.M. Stern's 1280 Fifth Gets Dressed for All Seasons," *Curbed*, November 16, 2010.
Lisa Delgado, "NYC's State of the Arts," *Oculus*, Fall 2010, 24–25.
S. Jhoanna Robledo, "Uptown Upturn," *New York*, February 14, 2011, 48.
Karrie Jacobs, "You Are Where You Live," *Dwell*, March 2011, 73.
Rachel Ohm, "Home at Last," *The New York Observer Magazine*, April 2011, 52–54.
Kate Taylor, "Museum for African Art Delays Opening," *The New York Times*, June 15, 2011, C:3.
Sara Polsky, "Robert A.M. Stern Parties at 1280 Fifth," *Curbed*, June 15, 2011.
Max Gross, "The Fifth Estates: Development Heads North of 96th Street," *New York Post*, August 18, 2011.
S. Jhoanna Robledo, "Topping Out? Developers Try to Push Fifth Avenue Luxury Past 96th Street," *New York*, August 8–15, 2011, 58.
Laura Kusisto, "Reaching High on Upper Fifth Avenue," *The Wall Street Journal*, October 21, 2011, A:20.
Robbie Whelan, "A Home for Art That's Outside the Box," *The Wall Street Journal*, December 5, 2011, A:24.
Claire Wilson, "Museum Mile Makeover," *Oculus*, Spring 2012, 21.
David Kaufman, "Take the Fifth: Will Manhattan Buyers Be Lured North of 96th Street?" *Financial Times*, December 10–11, 2011, House & Home: 3.
Alexei Barrionuevo, "Goodbye Malaria, Hello Condos," *The New York Times*, March 25, 2012, Real Estate: 1, 4.
Josh Barbanel, "Condo Building Goes Extra Distance," *The Wall Street Journal*, April 10, 2012, A:22.
Sara Polsky, "1280 Fifth Avenue Plans to Relaunch Sales Under New Name," *Curbed*, April 10, 2012.

Joyce Cohen, "A Three-Bedroom; Anywhere Is Fine," *The New York Times,* June 3, 2012, Real Estate: 1, 4.

Rob Bear, "Five Missteps by the Vaunted Architect Robert A.M. Stern," *Curbed,* December 11, 2012.

Barbara Thau, "Movin' On Up," *New York Cottages & Gardens,* March 2013, 52, 54.

Jennifer Maloney, "Museum Pivots Toward Policy," *The Wall Street Journal,* August 23, 2013, A:15, 20.

Patricia Cohen, "Museum for African Art Broadens Its Mandate," *The New York Times,* August 24, 2013, C:3.

Jennifer Maloney, "New Africa Center's Journey in N.Y.," *The Wall Street Journal,* September 28–29, 2013, A:19.

Nancy Keates, "A (Museum) Mile in Their Shoes," *The Wall Street Journal,* June 13, 2014, M:3.

Patricia Cohen, "When a Museum's Big Dreams Prove Too Ambitious," *The New York Times,* July 23, 2013, C:1.

The Century
Los Angeles, California

Partner: Sargent C. Gardiner, Daniel Lobitz, Paul L. Whalen. Senior Associate: Victoria Baran. Associates: Johnny Cruz, Enid De Gracia, Mike Soriano. Team: Merced Baumer, Seher Erdogan, Peter Garofalo, Bryan Hale, Miyun Kang, David Nguyen, Kurt Roessler. Interior Design Associate: John Boyland. Interior Design Assistants: Jana Happel, Lisa Koch, Alys Stephens. Associate Architect: HKS Architects. Landscape Architect: Pamela Burton and Company.

Robert A.M. Stern: Buildings and Projects 2004–2009 (New York: The Monacelli Press, 2009), 434–37.

"East Meets West," *Interior Design,* May 2010, 269.

Dakota Smith, "Related Decides to Drop Prices at the Century," *Curbed,* July 1, 2010.

Roger Vincent, "Luxury Condo tower in Century City Is Completed," *Los Angeles Times,* July 24, 2010.

Roger Vincent, "Condo Tower in Century City Joins the Rise of Luxe High-Rises," *Los Angeles Times,* July 24, 2010, B:1, 4.

Dakota Smith, "Candy Closes at the Century, Pays $35 Million for Penthouse," *Curbed,* December 8, 2010.

"L.A.'s Newest Luxury Properties Struggle Through a Lethargic Market," *The Hollywood Reporter,* February 25, 2011.

Bob Morris and Lauren Schumacher, "Urban Sanctuaries," *Robb Report Exceptional Properties,* September/October 2011, 58–62, 64.

"The Aesthetic Versatility of Precast," *Ascent,* Winter 2012, 28–31.

Morgan Brennan, "America's Most Amazing High-Rise Mansions," *Forbes,* March 8, 2012.

Alexei Barrionuevo, "Condo Dreams in a Mansion Town," *The New York Times,* May 6, 2012, Real Estate: 1, 4.

Lauren Schuker Blum, "Goodbye, Estate; Hello, Doorman," *The Wall Street Journal,* October 12, 2012, M:3.

Lisa Boone, "THR Design Hollywood at the Century: Step Inside Luxury High-Rise," *Los Angeles Times,* October 20, 2012.

Amy Schellenbaum, "Here Now, *The Hollywood Reporter's* First-Ever Showhouse," *Curbed,* October 24, 2012.

Degen Pener, "Hollywood's 25 Most Influential Interior Designers," *The Hollywood Reporter,* November 2, 2012, 56–69.

Degen Pener, "How to Create Design Drama in a Small Space: Secrets from the THR Showhouse," *The Hollywood Reporter,* November 16, 2012.

Alexandria Abramian, "Candy Spelling Set to Reveal $35 Million Manor in the Sky on HGTV," *The Hollywood Reporter,* August 9, 2013.

Bavaro Hall
Curry School of Education, University of Virginia, Charlottesville, Virginia

Partners: Preston J. Gumberich, Graham S. Wyatt. Project Manager: Connie Osborn. Team: Kanu Agrawal, Noel Angeles, Matthew Blumenthal, Emilia Ferri, Sean Foley, Megan Fullagar, Christopher Heim, Daniel Hogan, Stephanie Mena, George Punnoose, Janice Rivera-Hall, Michael Ryan, Yok Saowasang, Mike Soriano, Charles Toothill, Marek Turzynski. Interior Design Associate: Shannon Ratcliff. Interior Design Assistants: Philip Chan, Michelle Everett. Model Builder: David Abecassis. Landscape Architect: Ann P. Stokes Landscape Architects.

"Bravo Bavaro!" *Curry* (magazine of the University of Virginia Curry School of Education), Autumn 2006, cover, 13–17.

Robert A.M. Stern: Buildings and Projects 2004–2009 (New York: The Monacelli Press, 2009), 472–73.

"Dedication Ceremony Planned for U.Va.'s Bavaro Hall on Friday," *UVa Today,* July 14, 2010.

Brandon Shulleeta, "Building Bolsters UVa Education School," *The Daily Progress,* July 17, 2010, A:1, 10.

Robert A.M. Stern: On Campus (New York: The Monacelli Press, 2010), 16–22, 34–39.

North Hall and Library
Bronx Community College, The City University of New York, Bronx, New York

Partners: Augusta Barone, Alexander P. Lamis, Graham S. Wyatt. Senior Associates: Jeffery Povero, Dennis Sagiev. Associate: Kaveri Singh. Team: Tatyana Albinder, Natalie Goldberg, Zachary Heaps, William Holloway, Katherine LoBalbo, Erin Murphy, Alicia Reed, Michael Ryan, Dongju Seo, Michael Tabacinic. Interior Design Assistant: Philip Chan. Landscape Design Senior Associates: Kendra Taylor, Michael Weber. Landscape Design Project Managers: Joelle Byrer, Kevin Hasselwander. Landscape Design Assistants: Dan Evans, Noy Lamb. Model Builders: David Abecassis, Bruce Lindsay. Associate Architect: Ismael Leyva Architects.

Robert A.M. Stern: Buildings and Projects 2004–2009 (New York: The Monacelli Press, 2009), 478–79.

Robert A.M. Stern: On Campus (New York: The Monacelli Press, 2010), 108–11.

James Gardner, "Bronx Community College Deserves to Be—Architecturally Speaking—on the Map," *The Real Deal,* March 3, 2011.

Tanyanika Samuels, "Artist Captures Bronx Scenes on Canvas; Works Will Decorate New Building at Bronx Community College," *New York Daily News,* March 11, 2012.

"Glorious Panoramas of an Unsung Borough," *CUNY Matters,* Spring 2012, 4.

Lawrence Biemiller, "Bronx Community College Opens New Library," *The Chronicle of Higher Education,* September 4, 2012.

Liz Robbins, "Battered and Beautiful: His Bronx," *The New York Times,* September 30, 2012, Metro: 1, 8.

David W. Dunlap, "A Bronx College Gets a Library That Is Truly Its Own," *The New York Times,* September 3, 2013, A:15.

Nancy A. Ruhling, "Completing the Quadrangle," *Traditional Building,* April 2014, 16–19.

Alan B. Miller Hall
Mason School of Business, The College of William and Mary, Williamsburg, Virginia

Partners: Kevin M. Smith, Graham S. Wyatt. Project Manager: Lara Kailian. Team: Kanu Agrawal, Hee-Young Cho, Christopher Heim, Antonio Salvador, Saul Uranovsky. Interior Design Associate: Shannon Ratcliff. Interior Design

Assistants: Michelle Everett, Sandra Fayadel, Sam Mason, Mitra Moshari. Landscape Architect: Ann P. Stokes Architects. Associate Architect: Moseley Architects.

Robert A.M. Stern: Buildings and Projects 1999–2003 (New York: The Monacelli Press, 2003), 566.
Robert A.M. Stern: Buildings and Projects 2004–2009 (New York: The Monacelli Press, 2009), 498–99.
Carol Scheid, "Architectural Gem at W&M," *The Virginia Gazette*, August 29, 2009.
Jimmy Anuszewski, "Public-Private Partnerships: Financing Options for Your Project," *Owners Perspective*, Fall 2009, cover, 6–8.
Melissa V. Pinard, "Open for Business: Alan B. Miller Hall Serves as the New Home for the Mason School of Business," *William & Mary Alumni Magazine*, Winter 2009, cover, 38–41.
Lawrence Biemiller, "Matchy-Matchy Style: Enough Already, Your New Buildings Need Not Look Old," *The Chronicle of Higher Education*, May 21, 2010, B:1, 6–9.
Nancy A. Ruhling, "History Lessons," *Traditional Building*, June 2010, 22–24.
Robert Nieminen and Jamie Nicpon, "10 Top LEED Projects," *Interiors and Sources*, October/November 2010, 41–51.
Robert A.M. Stern: On Campus (New York: The Monacelli Press, 2010), 44–55.
Edwin Heathcote, "Outside the Box: New Architecture for Business Schools," *Financial Times*, January 31, 2011.

Our Lady of Mercy Chapel
Salve Regina University, Newport, Rhode Island

Partner: Grant F. Marani. Senior Associate: Charles Toothill. Associates: Goil Amornvivat, Megan St. Denis. Team: Mario Cruzate, Ken Frank, Ellee Lee, Megan St. Denis, Kayin Tse. Associate Architect: Richard W. Quinn, FAIA, and Newport Collaborative Architects.

Robert A.M. Stern: Buildings and Projects 2004–2009 (New York: The Monacelli Press, 2009), 502–3.
"Building on Faith," *Report from Newport*, Summer 2009, 4.
Robert A.M. Stern: On Campus (New York: The Monacelli Press, 2010), 364–67, 378–87.
David Brussat, "Roses and Raspberries for 2010," *The Providence Journal*, January 6, 2011.
Jill Connors, "A Vernacular Hymn," *Design New England*, May/June 2011, 48–52.
Robert A.M. Stern, "Chapel for a Queen," *Faith & Form*, 1/2012, 16–17.
Martha McDonald, "Shingle Gem," *Traditional Building*, June 2012, 30–33.
Diane Holliday, "Our Lady of Mercy Chapel," *Historic Houses*, August 27, 2012.

Superior Ink
New York, New York

Partners: Michael D. Jones, Paul L. Whalen. Project Manager: Robert HuDock. Team: Aaron Boucher, Adrian Coleman, Clarisa Diaz, Russell Grant, Stuart Johnson, Michael Leocata, Chen-Huan Liao, Ulises Liceaga, David Nguyen, Kurt Roessler. Associate Architect: Ismael Levya Architects, PC. Interior Designer: Yabu Pushelberg.

Robert A.M. Stern: Buildings and Projects 2004–2009 (New York: The Monacelli Press, 2009), 516–21.
Joey Arak, "25 Million Reasons Why Superior Ink Is Doing Just Fine," *Curbed*, October 1, 2009.
Joey Arak, "Superior Ink Makes Bid for World Domination," *Curbed*, December 17, 2009.
Norval White and Elliott Wilensky, *AIA Guide to New York City*, fifth edition (Oxford University Press, 2010), 169.

Pete Davies, "Marc Jacobs Is Russian to Complete His Superior Townhouse," *Curbed*, April 13, 2010.
Candace Taylor, "Hitting the Magic Number," *The Real Deal*, April 2010, 38, 87.
Marc Santora, "Town Houses With Benefits," *The New York Times*, September 5, 2010, Real Estate: 1, 9.
Arthur Lubow, "The Traditionalist," *The New York Times Magazine*, October 17, 2010, 68–71.
Sarabeth Sanders, "Related's Boss Nabs a Superior Ink Pad," *The Real Deal*, November 29, 2010.
Anne Field, "Starchitects Pay Off Big," *Crain's New York Business*, November 28, 2011, 15, 18.
Celia Barbour, "Manhattan Transfer," *Elle Décor*, December 2011, 126–31.
Marc Santora, "Buy: The Ultraluxury Market Barely Missed a Beat in the Recession," *The New York Times*, February 12, 2012, Real Estate: 1, 8.
Alexei Barrionuevo, "Trophy Hunting in Manhattan," *The New York Times*, June 10, 2012, Real Estate: 1, 4.
Dan Shaw, "No Boundaries," *Architectural Digest*, July 2012, 104–11.
Hana R. Alberts, "Some of 2013's Most Expensive Buildings Will Surprise You," *Curbed*, January 23, 2014.

Christoverson Humanities Building
Florida Southern College, Lakeland, Florida

Partner: Alexander P. Lamis. Senior Associate: Jeffery Povero. Associates: Roland Flores, James Pearson, Salvador Peña-Figueroa, Sara Rubenstein, Susan Ryder. Team: Doreen Adengo, Gali Osterweil, Anthony Polito, Vanessa Sanchez, Daniel Siegle, Addie Suchorab. Interior Design Associate: Hyung Kee Lee. Associate Architect: Wallis Murphey Boyington Architects.

Robert A.M. Stern: Buildings and Projects 2004–2009 (New York: The Monacelli Press, 2009), 492–93.
Robert A.M. Stern: On Campus (New York: The Monacelli Press, 2010), 234–37.
Saxon Henry, "A New Dawn for Wright's Child of the Sun," *Modernism*, Spring 2010, 60–69.
Cary McMullen, "New Addition to FSC Echoes Wright's Motifs," *The Ledger*, November 12, 2010.
"*Princeton Review*: FSC's Campus One of the Nation's Most Beautiful," *Southern News*, Winter 2010.
"Christoverson Humanities Building a Splendid Addition to FSC Campus," *Southern News*, Winter 2011, cover, 12.

North Quad Residential and Academic Complex
University of Michigan, Ann Arbor, Michigan

Partners: Preston J. Gumberich, Graham S. Wyatt. Senior Associate: Jeffery Povero. Associate: George Punnoose. Project Managers: Sean Foley, Bradley Gay, Celeste Hall. Team: Kanu Agrawal, Daniel Arbelaez, Fredric Berthelot, Hee-Young Cho, Kathryn Everett, Megan Fullagar, Stephanie Mena, Connie Osborn, William Perez, Yok Saowasang, Dongju Seo, Sue Jin Sung, Michael Tabacinic. Interior Design Assistant: Philip Chan. Model Builder: David Abecassis. Landscape Architect: Pollack Design Associates. Associate Architect: Einhorn Yaffee Prescott Architecture & Engineering.

Robert A.M. Stern: Buildings and Projects 2004–2009 (New York: The Monacelli Press, 2009), 272–73.
Robert A.M. Stern: On Campus (New York: The Monacelli Press, 2010), 324–28, 338–45.
Preston Gumberich, "North Quad 24/7: Unanimous Vote for Hand-Molded Brick Ensures Integrity of Campus' Architectural Heritage," *Masonry Edge and The Story Pole*, Vol. 4, No. 4 (2010), 34–37.
"North Quad: New Campus Landmark Blends Academics and Residential Life," *Leaders & Best: Philanthropy at Michigan*, Summer 2010, cover, 10–11.

Lori Horwedel, "University of Michigan's $175 Million North Quad Complex Ready for Students," *Ann Arbor*, August 5, 2010.
"Spotlight: University of Michigan," *Talking Stick*, September/October 2010, 8.
Cathy Mizgerd, "Built to Last," *Leaders & Best: Philanthropy at Michigan*, Fall 2011, cover, 10–11.

East Hampton Town Hall
East Hampton, New York

Partner: Randy M. Correll. Project Manager: Christian N. Dickson. Team: Aiyla Balakumar, Hannah Cho, Wing Poon, Caroline Graf Statile, Todd Sullivan, Hillary Tate. Interior Design Project Manager: Marissa Savarese. Landscape Design Senior Associate: Kendra Taylor.

Robert A.M. Stern: Buildings and Projects 2004–2009 (New York: The Monacelli Press, 2009), 589.
Joanne Pilgrim, "New-Old Town Hall Use Unclear," *The East Hampton Star*, January 21, 2010, A:1, 11.
Dan Rattiner, "If It's Not Going to Be a Town Hall, What Do You Suggest It Be?" *Dan's Papers*, January 22, 2010.
Zak Powers, *Further Lane* (The Quantuck Lane Press, 2011).
Jennifer Landes, "Chronicling a Historic Move From Dunes to Town," *The East Hampton Star*, April 28, 2011, C:1, 3.
Julie Iovine, "Town Hall Assembly," *The Wall Street Journal*, October 12, 2011, D:5.
Eve M. Kahn, "A Photographic Story," *Traditional Building*, December 2011, 94.
Lamar Clarkson, "East Hampton Town Hall," *Architectural Record*, February 2012.
Michael J. Crosbie, "East Hampton Town Hall," *Architecture Week*, April 18, 2012.

House in Sonoma Valley
Glen Ellen, California

Partner: Grant F. Marani. Associate: Megan St Denis. Project Manager: Danny Chiang. Team: Lauren Bollettino, Esther Park. Landscape Design Senior Associate: Kendra Taylor. Landscape Design Assistant: Terrie Gamble. Interior Designer: Agnes Bourne.

Designs for Living: Houses by Robert A.M. Stern Architects (New York: The Monacelli Press, 2014), 340–65.
"Poet's Retreat: Grant Marani, Partner at Robert A.M. Stern Architects, Designs an Intimate Hilltop Haven," *San Francisco Cottages & Gardens*, May 2014, 78–83.

Chapel Hill Public Library
Chapel Hill, North Carolina

Partners: Alexander P. Lamis, Kevin M. Smith. Associates: James Pearson, Sara Rubenstein, Susan Ryder. Project Manager: Gali Osterweil. Team: Vanessa Sanchez, Addie Suchorab. Associate Architect: Corley Redfoot Architects. Landscape Architect: OBS Landscape Architects

Robert A.M. Stern: Buildings and Projects 2004–2009 (New York: The Monacelli Press, 2009), 591.
Sarah Mansur, "Library On Time and On Budget," *The Chapel Hill News*, July 21, 2012.
Marissa Bane, "Chapel Hill Library to Reopen in April," *The Daily Tar Heel*, January 17, 2013.
Anne Brenner, "After a Decade, CH Opens New Public Library," *Chapelboro*, April 20, 2013.

Mas Fleuri
St.-Jean-Cap-Ferrat, France

Partner: Grant F. Marani. Associate: Rosa Maria Colina. Project Manager: Peter Lombardi-Krieps. Team: Lauren Bollettino, Brian Fell, Esther Park. Interior

Design Associate: John Boyland. Interior Design Assistants: Alexandra Rolland, Aruni Weerasinghe. Landscape Design Senior Associate: Kendra Taylor. Landscape Design Assistant: Meredith Lawson. Associate Architect: Lino Barone / Studio Laura Tibald.

House in Southampton
Southampton, New York

Partner: Randy M. Correll. Project Managers: Pamela McGinn, Caroline Graf Statile. Team: Hannah Cho, Nicholas DeRosa. Interior Designer: Liliane Peck. Landscape Architect: LaGuardia Design.

Maisonette in Chicago
Chicago, Illinois

Partner: Randy M. Correll. Project Manager: Craig Stevens. Team: Allen Philip Robinson. Interior Designer: Arthur Dunnam of Jed Johnson Associates.

Lisa Skolnik, "Coming Home," *Luxe*, Winter 2012, 218–27.
Designs for Living: Houses by Robert A.M. Stern Architects (New York: The Monacelli Press, 2014), 156–77.

18 Gramercy Park
New York, New York

Partners: Michael D. Jones, Paul L. Whalen. Senior Associates: Victoria Baran, Hernan Chebar. Associate: Gerard Beekman. Project Manager: Roberto Burneo. Team: Armando Amaral, Laura Boutwell, Russell Grant, Franklin Nunez, Jin Park. Interior Design Partner: Alexander P. Lamis. Interior Design Associate: John Boyland. Interior Design Assistants: Ann Baumgartner, Bennet Liefer, Aruni Weerasinghe. Associate Architect: John Schimenti, P.C.

Robert A.M. Stern: Buildings and Projects 2004–2009 (New York: The Monacelli Press, 2009), 594.
Lois Weiss, "18 Gramercy Finds Salvation," *New York Post*, August 11, 2010, 32.
Joey Arak, "15 Central Park West Dream Team Reunites in Gramercy Park," *Curbed*, August 11, 2010.
Joey Arak, "Transformation of Gramercy Park's Tower o' Ladies Begins," *Curbed*, January 27, 2011.
Fred A. Bernstein, "Once Institutional, Now Exclusive," *The New York Times*, January 22, 2012, Real Estate: 1, 8.
Josh Barbanel, "Zeckendorfs Swing for Hit at Another Park," *The Wall Street Journal*, July 11, 2012, A:18.
Holly Dunton, "Zeckendorfs Eye Another Home-Run With 18 GPS," *Real Estate Weekly*, September 27, 2012.
Robin Finn, "That's Some Key," *The New York Times*, September 30, 2012, Real Estate: 1, 8.
Josh Barbanel and Craig Karmin, "Gramercy Park Condo Goes Into Contract for $42 Million," *The Wall Street Journal*, October 5, 2012, M:2.
Kim Velsey, "18 Gramercy Park Is Having the Best Fall Ever," *The New York Observer*, October 18, 2012.
Meredith Galante, "Inside the Glitzy New Gramercy Park Building That's Selling Out Before It's Even Completed," *Business Insider*, October 25, 2012.
Max Gross, "Gramercy Spark: How Do You Follow the Record-Setting 15 Central Park West? Here's How," *New York Post*, November 15, 2012, 47, 50.
Haley Friedlich, "Brother Act," *Avenue*, December 2012, 82–83.
"Gramercy Chic," *New York Cottages & Gardens*, April 2013, 47.
C.J. Hughes, "All Keyed Up: Are the Zeckendorf Brothers and Robert A.M. Stern Creating the Magic of 15 Central Park West on Gramercy Park?" *Gotham Magazine*, Vol. 13, No. 6 (2013), 105–6.
Guelde Voien, "18 Gramercy Park Ranked Highest-Priced New Project of 2013," *The Real Deal*, January 7, 2014.

Angela Hunt, "Big Name Buyers Opt for Small Luxury Buildings," *The Real Deal*, January 21, 2014.

Hana R. Alberts, "Some of 2013's Most Expensive Buildings Will Surprise You," *Curbed*, January 23, 2014.

50 Connaught Road, Central
Hong Kong

Partner: Paul L. Whalen. Senior Associates: Hernan Chebar, David Winterton. Team: Armando Amaral, Josh Barkan, Franklin Nunez, Jin Park, Camellia Tian. Associate Architect: Aedas Ltd.

Robert A.M. Stern: Buildings and Projects 2004–2009 (New York: The Monacelli Press, 2009), 550–51.

Rosie Gogan-Keogh, "New York State of Mind," *Hong Kong Tatler*, September 2011, 228–33.

Pavan Shamdasani, "Past Pleasures," *South China Morning Post*, November 2011, 34–37.

Yoko Choy, "White Cube Opens a Hong Kong Gallery," *Wallpaper**, April 2012.

Yvonne Liu, "Central Building Sold for HK$4.88b," *South China Morning Post*, May 9, 2012.

Cindy Lee, "Grade A Office Building No. 50 Connaught Road Central Sold for HK$4.88 Billion," *Bloomberg*, May 15, 2012.

Robert Carr, "Chinese Bank Buys Hong Kong Tower for $629 Million," *Globe St.*, May 15, 2012.

Uncommon Charter and Achievement First High Schools
Brooklyn, New York

Partners: Augusta Barone, Melissa DelVecchio, Graham S. Wyatt. Senior Associate: Dennis Sagiev. Team: Jennifer Bailey, Timothy Carroll, Kathryn Everett, Bradley Gay, Natalie Goldberg, Isabel Gonzalez, Christopher Heim, Silas Jeffrey, Jennifer Lee, Anthony McConnell, Michael Ryan, William West. Model Builder: Tehniyet Masood. Interior Design Associate: Philip Chan. Interior Design Assistants: Shannon Ratcliff, Alexandra Rolland. Associate Architect: Gensler. Interior Designer: Gensler.

Robert A.M. Stern: Buildings and Projects 2004–2009 (New York: The Monacelli Press, 2009), 552–53.

30 Park Place
Four Season Private Residences, New York Downtown, New York, New York

Partners: Sargent C. Gardiner, Daniel Lobitz, Paul L. Whalen. Associates: Kyung Sook Gemma Kim, Tad Roemer, Kley Salas. Team: Adrian Coleman, Johnny Cruz, Laura Greenberg, Saul Hayutin, Ricardo Kendall, Matt Lynch, Rebecca Morgan, Benjamin Myers, Jonathan Palmer-Hoffman, Kurt Roessler, Benjamin Salling, Hilary Tate. Interior Design Partner: Alexander P. Lamis. Interior Design Associate: John Boyland. Interior Design Assistants: Ross Alexander, Marissa Savareese, Aruni Weerasinghe. Associate Architect: SLCE Architects. Interior Designers (hotel): Yabu Pushelburg. Landscape Architect: Lee Weintraub Landscape Architects.

Robert A.M. Stern: Buildings and Projects 2004–2009 (New York: The Monacelli Press, 2009), 554–57.

Norval White and Elliott Wilensky, *AIA Guide to New York City*, fifth edition (Oxford University Press, 2010), 85.

Eliot Brown, "Condo-Hotel Tower Aims for Superluxury," *The Wall Street Journal*, May 15, 2013, A:19.

Sara Polsky, "The World Is Finally Ready for Larry Silverstein's 30 Park Place," *Curbed*, May 15, 2013.

Nicole Anderson, "Stalled Residential Tower in Lower Manhattan to Rise Next to Woolworth Building," *The Architect's Newspaper*, May 15, 2013.

Charles V. Bagli, "Sky High and Going Up Fast: Luxury Towers Take New York," *The New York Times*, May 19, 2013, 1, 16.

Carl Yost, "Are Billionaires Ruining the New York Skyline? An Exhibition Examines the New Luxury Tower," *Architizer*, October 30, 2013.

Max Gross, "High FiDi: Luxury Real Estate in the Shadow of Wall Street," *New York Post*, November 21, 2013, 42.

Catherine Yang, "30 Park Place: Tallest Downtown Residential Tower Under Construction," *The Epoch Times*, December 3, 2013.

"Silverstein Starts Work on Four Seasons Tower," *Real Estate Weekly*, December 6, 2013.

Lois Weiss, "Room, Vroom! Slick New NYC Hotels Are Opening Fast and Furiously," *New York Post*, December 10, 2013, 42.

Claire Wilson, "Financial District Turns Touristy," *Oculus*, Winter 2013, 18.

C.J. Hughes, "In High Gear," *The New York Times*, April 27, 2014, Real Estate: 1, 12.

James Gardner, "30 Park Place: A Nod to a Masterpiece," *The Real Deal*, May 2014, 82.

Jessica Dailey, "Here Now, the First Floorplans of Silverstein's 30 Park Place," *Curbed*, May 9, 2014.

Josh Barbanel, "Condos Stack Up Downtown," *The Wall Street Journal*, May 17–18, 2014, A:15, 18.

Jessica Dailey, "Long-Awaited 30 Park Place Reveals Condo Interiors," *Curbed*, May 21, 2014.

"Sales Get Underway at Silverstein's 30 Park," *Real Estate Weekly*, June 5, 2014.

Lois Weiss, "Reach for the Sky," *New York Post*, June 8, 2014, 28–29.

Katherine Clarke, "He's Good Copy: Stern's Design Cloned All Over," *New York Daily News*, June 20, 2014, Real Estate: 1–2.

Sasha van Oldershausen, "Luxury Condo Overload?" *The Real Deal*, July 2014, 71–72.

George W. Bush Presidential Center
Southern Methodist University, Dallas, Texas

Partners: Augusta Barone, Alexander P. Lamis, Graham S. Wyatt. Senior Associates: Jennifer Stone, Charles Toothill. Associates: Enid De Gracia, Thomas Lewis, Salvador Peña-Figueroa, James Pearson, Susan Ryder, Paul Zembsch. Team: Seher Aziz, Jennifer Bailey, Elizabeth Bondaryk, Deirdre Cerminaro, Danny Chiang, Adrian Coleman, Mario Cruzate, Jorge Fontan, Megan Fullagar, Anya Grant, Milton Hernandez, Ruth Irving, Hussam Jallad, Bradley Jones, Emily Jones, Kathryn Lenehan, Miyun Kang, Peter Lombardi-Krieps, Mako Maeno, Mary Martinich, Anthony McConnell, Rebecca Morgan, Wing Yee Ng Fung-Fortugno, Jung-Yoon Park, Gali Osterweil, Jung-Yoon Park, William Perez, Karen Rizvi, Tadam Roemer, Nasheet Rumy, Vanessa Sanchez, Jessica Saniewski, Daniel Siegel, Heather Spigner, Addie Suchorab, Yoko Suzuki, William Work, Albert Yadao, Charles Yoo, Young Jin Yoon. Interior Design Associates: John Boyland, Philip Chan, Lawrence Chabra. Interior Design Associates: Kelsi Swank, Christine Kang. Model Builders: David Abecassis, Seth Burney, Bruce Lindsay, Victor Marcelino. Landscape Architect: Michael Van Valkenburgh Associates.

Robert A.M. Stern: Buildings and Projects 2004–2009 (New York: The Monacelli Press, 2009), 576–77.

Lori Stahl, "Laura Bush Enthusiastic About Landscape Architect for Presidential Library," *The Dallas Morning News*, January 28, 2009.

James Traub, "George Bush's Plans for His Presidential Center at S.M.U. Are Controversial Even Before Ground Has Been Broken," *The New York Times Magazine*, March 15, 2009, 40–43.

"Robert A.M. Stern, Part 1," *ArchiTakes*, September 17, 2009.

David Dillon, "Bush Library Building Plays Off Its Environs at SMU," *The Dallas Morning News*, November 18, 2009, A:1, 14.

Lori Stahl, "Laura Bush: Library Not a Monument but a Showcase," *The Dallas Morning News*, November 18, 2009, A:1, 14.

Christopher Hawthorne, "Little Swagger in Plans for Bush Presidential Library," *Los Angeles Times,* November 18, 2009.

David Jackson, "Presidential Center Plans Thrill Bushes," *USA Today,* November 18, 2009, A:1, 5.

Lori Stahl, "Freedom Stars in Bush Library," *The Dallas Morning News,* November 19, 2009, B:1, 9.

Anna M. Tinsley, "Bush Complex Will Have a Thoroughly Texas Look," *Star-Telegram,* November 19, 2009, A:1.

Amir Sharif, "Bush Library Plans Unveiled," *Yale Daily News,* November 19, 2009, 1, 3.

"Design Is Revealed for Bush Center," *The New York Times,* November 19, 2009, C:2.

Alissa Walker, "What Do Presidential Libraries Say About Their Namesakes' Legacies?" *Fast Company,* November 20, 2009.

Philip Kennicott, "A Presidential Library With Modest Virtues," *The Washington Post,* November 21, 2009, C:1, 4.

David Dillon, "Robert A.M. Stern Unveils Design for Bush Library," *Architectural Record,* November 23, 2009.

"Flags, Yes, but No Fluted Columns," *The Chronicle of Higher Education,* November 27, 2009, A:3.

Leonard Kniffel, "Bush Presidential Library Unveiled; Design Goes for the Green," *American Libraries,* January / February 2010, 18.

Randy Lee Loftis, "George W. Bush Presidential Library's Blueprints Filled With Green, Following Trend of Other Big Public Buildings," *The Dallas Morning News,* March 14, 2010.

Tom Benning, "Bush Library Plans Oval Office, Considers 9/11 Artifacts," *The Dallas Morning News,* May 30, 2010.

Bill Hethcock, "George W. Bush Presidential Library Details Revealed," *Dallas Business Journal,* June 24, 2010.

Taylor Adams, "Breaking Ground: SMU Prepares for the George W. Bush Presidential Center," *The Daily Campus,* November 15, 2010, 1, 3.

Ana Campoy, "Bookend to a Presidency," *The Wall Street Journal,* November 17, 2010.

Peter Baker, "Bush and Cheney, Together Again at Groundbreaking," *The New York Times,* November 17, 2010, A:18.

"George W. Bush Presidential Center Stays Loyal to Texas With Local Materials," *Building Design + Construction,* December 2010, 15.

Robert A.M. Stern: On Campus (New York: The Monacelli Press, 2010), 124–35.

Nate Eudaly, "Building Sustainably to Preserve History: Presidential Libraries and the George W. Bush Center," *Columns,* Spring 2011, 16–19.

Tom Benning, "George W. Bush Presidential Center to Mark Milestone," *The Dallas Morning News,* October 1, 2011.

Tom Benning, "Guests to Get Sneak Peek at Bush Library," *The Dallas Morning News,* October 2, 2011, 1, 5.

Anna M. Tinsley, "Bush Says Progress on His Presidential Center Is Awe-Inspiring," *Star-Telegram,* October 3, 2011.

Tom Benning, "Glimpse of Things to Come," *The Dallas Morning News,* December 4, 2011, 1, 7.

Debra Wood, "Bush Presidential Center Pushes Energy Efficiency," *Engineering News-Record,* June 11, 2012.

The SMU Campus at 100 (Southern Methodist University, 2012), 94.

Nicholas Sakelaris, "Bush Center Blends History, Modern Design," *Dallas Business Journal,* April 5, 2013.

Mark Lamster, "The George W. Bush Presidential Center," *The Dallas Morning News,* April 20, 2013.

Peter Baker, "With Grandchild and Library, a New Chapter for Bush," *The New York Times,* April 16, 2013, A:16.

Christopher Hawthorne, "Bush Presidential Library Is Fittingly Blunt," *Los Angeles Times,* April 20, 2013.

Mark Lamster, "Architect Robert A.M. Stern on the George W. Bush Presidential Center," *The Dallas Morning News,* April 21, 2013.

Peter Baker, "Rewinding History, Bush Museum Lets You Decide," *The New York Times,* April 21, 2013, A:1, 16.

"George W. Bush to Dedicate His Presidential Library Today," *Parade,* April 25, 2013.

Henry Grabar, "An Architectural Reflection of George W. Bush," *The Atlantic Cities,* April 25, 2013.

Peter Baker, "For Bush, a Day to Bask in Texas Sun," *The New York Times,* April 26, 2013, A:10, 23.

Sharon McHugh, "Robert A.M. Stern Building Complete," *World Architecture News,* April 26, 2013.

Julie V. Iovine, "Bricks and Immortality," *The Wall Street Journal,* April 30, 2013, D:5.

Ingrid Spencer, "The George W. Bush Presidential Center," *Architectural Record,* May 2013, 42.

Katie Gerfen, "George W. Bush Presidential Center," *Architect,* May 2013, 110–17.

Paul Goldberger, "On Not Hating the New George W. Bush Library," *Vanity Fair,* May 24, 2013.

Margaret Russell, "Editor's Page," *Architectural Digest,* June 2013, 34.

William Middleton, "Presidential Statement," *Architectural Digest,* June 2013, 63–64, 66.

Douglas Brinkley, "A Showcase of George W. Bush's Greatest Achievements," *Newsmax,* May 2013, 50–56.

"Robert A.M. Stern, George W. Bush Presidential Center in Dallas," *Arquitectura Viva,* September 15, 2013.

Maarten Girlen and Lionel Devlieger, "Sustainable," *Abitare,* September / October 2013, 74–75.

Barbara Horwitz-Bennett, "First Line of Defense," *Net Zero Building,* November 2013, 10.

Michael Malone, "It's George, Not Georgian," *Texas Architect,* November / December 2013, 54–61.

Frederick Steiner, "The Necessity of Constraints," *Topos,* No. 83 (2013), 78–83.

Lyric W. Winik, ed., *The George W. Bush Presidential Center: A Celebration of Freedom* (George W. Bush Presidential Center, 2013).

Witold Rybczynski, "Obama and His Library: Go Small," *The New York Times,* February 19, 2014, A:19.

Marshall Brown, "Possibilities Over Prescriptions," *Metropolis,* May 2014, 64–70.

Thomas Frank, "The Animatronic Presidency," *Salon,* July 13, 2014.

Tour Carpe Diem
La Défense, Courbevoie, France

Partners: Meghan L. McDermott, Kevin M. Smith, Graham S. Wyatt. Associates: Fredric Berthelot, Renaud Magnaval. Team: Rebecca Atkin, Anya Grant, Milton Hernandz, Trevor Laubenstein, Douglas Neri, Kaveri Singh, Charles Yoo, Young Jin Yoon. Associate Architect: SRA Architectes. Interior Designer: Jean Jegou. Landscape Architect: Mutabilis.

Robert A.M. Stern: Buildings and Projects 2004–2009 (New York: The Monacelli Press, 2009), 558–63.

Frédérique Vergne, "Pose de la première pierre de la tour Carpe Diem à La Défense," *Le Moniteur,* March 14, 2011.

"Carpe Diem, 1ère tour française certifiée LEED et Platinum," *Le Moniteur,* April 4, 2013.

"Tour Carpe Diem," *Hinesight,* May/August 2013, 9.

Isabelle Duffaure-Gallais, "Une nouvelle tour dans le ciel de La Défense," *Le Moniteur,* May 24, 2013.

"La tour Carpe Diem signe le renouveau de La Défense," *Le Moniteur,* August 16, 2013.

"Inauguration de Carpe Diem, un grate-ciel écolo à La Défense," *Libération,* September 18, 2013.

Amel Brahmi-Howton, "Robert Stern, un Américain à La Défense," *Le Parisien,* September 24, 2013, V:1.

441

Marc Sautereau, "La Tour réinventée," *Centralités*, September 2013, cover, 26–27.

Catherine Sabbah, "Joëlle Chauvin: La promotion immobilière en questions," *Centralités*, September 2013, 47–51.

Enissa Bergevin, *Les 101 Mots de la Tour Carpe Diem: A l'usage de tous* (Archibooks, 2013).

"World's Best New Skyscraper Is ..." *CNN Travel*, May 20, 2014.

Florence Hubin, "Thalès va emménager dans la tour Carpe Diem," *Le Parisien*, June 3, 2014.

Hancock Center
Marist College, Poughkeepsie, New York

Partners: Kevin M. Smith, Graham S. Wyatt. Associate: Fredric Berthelot. Project Manager: Bram Janaitis. Project Designer: Michael Ryan. Team: Noel Angeles, Rebecca Atkin, Matthew Blumenthal, Isabel Gonzalez, Celeste Hall, Christopher Heim, Silas Jeffrey, Seema Malik, Ian Mills Dongju Seo. Interior Design Project Manager: Philip Chan. Interior Design Assistant: Tina Hu. Landscape Design Senior Associate: Michael Weber. Landscape Design Project Manager: Mark Rodriguez. Landscape Design Assistants: Joelle Byrer, Meredith Lawton, Demetrios Saturinos.

Robert A.M. Stern: Buildings and Projects 2004–2009 (New York: The Monacelli Press, 2009), 564–65.

Robert A.M. Stern: On Campus (New York: The Monacelli Press, 2010), 538–45.

Craig Wolf, "Marist Celebrates $35 Million Academic Hall," *Poughkeepsie Journal*, May 6, 2011.

Ron Treister, "American Stone Adds Character at Marist College," *Stone World*, July 2011, 142, 144, 146.

"Marist College, Poughkeepsie, New York," *Landscape Architect*, June 2014, 46–52.

Campus Gates and Pedestrian Crossing
Marist College, Poughkeepsie, New York

Partners: Kevin M. Smith, Graham S. Wyatt. Project Manager: Benjamin Salling. Team: Alexander Boardman, Christopher Heim. Associate Architect: New York State Department of Transportation. Landscape Architect: Imbiano Quigley Landscape Architects.

Robert A.M. Stern: Buildings and Projects 2004–2009 (New York: The Monacelli Press, 2009), 598.

Robert A.M. Stern: On Campus (New York: The Monacelli Press, 2010), 538–41.

Myles Williams, "Walkway Under Route 9 Makes Passage Safer for Students, Faster for Vehicles," *Marist Magazine*, Winter 2011/2102, 2.

"Marist College, Poughkeepsie, New York," *Landscape Architect*, June 2014, 46–52.

Residence in East Quogue
East Quogue, New York

Partner: Gary L. Brewer. Associate: Winnie Yen. Team: Terrie Gamble, C. Callaway Hayles, Scott Hirshson, Nicholas DeRosa, Michael Weber. Interior Designer: S.R. Gambrel, Inc. Landscape Architect: Edmund D. Hollander Landscape Architect Design P.C.

Designs for Living: Houses by Robert A.M. Stern Architects (New York: The Monacelli Press, 2014), 367–95.

Dan Shaw, "Winning Combination," *Architectural Digest*, June 2014, 112–19.

"The Summer Homes of Robert A.M. Stern Architects," *Dering Hall*, June 24, 2014.

520 Park Avenue
New York, New York

Partners: Michael D. Jones, Paul L. Whalen. Project Managers: Carlos Hurtado, David Rinehart. Team: Matthew Blumenthal, Hannah Cho, Ed Hsu, Adele Lim, Jin Park, Natalie Pierro, Tad Roemer, Leo Stevens. Interior Design Associate: John Boyland. Interior Design Assistant: Devin Borden. Landscape Design Senior Associate: Michael Weber. Landscape Design Assistant: Stephen Koren. Associate Architect: SLCE Architects.

"Sticking With Stern," *The Wall Street Journal*, December 19, 2012, C:11.

Charles V. Bagli, "$40 Million in Air Rights Will Let East Side Tower Soar," *The New York Times*, February 26, 2013, A:18.

Charles V. Bagli, "A Bigger Billionaires' Row With Central Park Views," *The New York Times*, October 16, 2013, A:21.

Hana R. Alberts, "Zeckendorf Says New Project Is Like a 15 Central Park West," *Curbed*, November 20, 2013.

The Accidental Skyline (The Municipal Art Society of New York), December 2013.

Jan Ransom and Matt Chaban, "Developers Are Turning Central Park Into Central Dark With Mega-Thin Towers," *New York Daily News*, December 25, 2013.

Josh Barbanel, "New, Traditional Tower Joins Billionaires Row," *The Wall Street Journal*, March 25, 2014, A:17, 20.

Kim Velsey, "Stern vs. Stern: Robert A.M. to Design Dueling Limestone Luxury Towers," *The New York Observer*, March 25, 2014.

"Robert A.M. Stern Tops NYC Tower With $100 Million Penthouse," *ArchDaily*, March 26, 2014.

Paul Goldberger, "Too Rich, Too Thin, Too Tall?" *Vanity Fair*, May 2014, 170–76.

Katherine Clarke, "He's Good Copy: Stern's Design Cloned All Over," *New York Daily News*, June 20, 2014, Real Estate: 1–2.

Tiffany Jewel Salon
New York, New York

Partner: Paul L. Whalen. Project Manager: Gerard Beekman. Team: Ed Hsu, Miyun Kang, Jonathan Pettibone, Chris Sowers. Interior Design Associate: John Boyland. Interior Design Assistant: Shannon Ratcliff.

Stellene Volandes, "The New Salon Privés," *Departures*, November 2010, 100, 102.

Isabelle Kellogg, "The King of Diamonds," *Connecticut Cottages & Gardens*, November 2012, 38, 40.

New College House
Franklin & Marshall College, Lancaster, Pennsylvania

Partners: Preston J. Gumberich, Graham S. Wyatt. Project Manager: Sean Foley. Team: George de Brigard, Kevin Fitzgerald, Melanie Fox, Milton Hernandez, Jennifer Lee, Thomas Lewis, Sung Chan Park, David Rinehart, Mike Soriano, Rosalind Tsang, Young Jin Yoon. Interior Design Associate: Shannon Ratcliff. Interior Design Assistants: Philip Chan, Sandra Fadayel, Ann Johnson, Crystal Palleschi. Model Builder: David Abecassis, Bruce Lindsay. Landscape Architect: OLIN.

Robert A.M. Stern: Buildings and Projects 2004–2009 (New York: The Monacelli Press, 2009), 570–71.

Lawrence Biemiller, "At Franklin & Marshall, Another New Building by Charles Z. Klauder," *The Chronicle of Higher Education*, October 19, 2009.

David Schuyler, "F&M's New Buildings Do Not Slavishly Copy Klauder's Work," *The Chronicle of Higher Education*, November 15, 2009.

Robert A.M. Stern: On Campus (New York: The Monacelli Press, 2010), 198–201.

Scott Carlson, "The College President as Urban Planner," *The Chronicle of Higher Education*, January 29, 2010, 1, 16–18.

Bernard Harris, "F&M Details Ambitious Goals," *Intelligencer Journal*, February 4, 2010, A:1, 4.

Lawrence Biemiller, "Matchy-Matchy Style: Enough Already, Your New Buildings Need Not Look Old," *The Chronicle of Higher Education*, May 21, 2010, B:1, 6–9.

East Campus Master Plan and Caruthers Biotechnology Building
University of Colorado Boulder, Boulder, Colorado

Partners: Sargent C. Gardiner, Paul L. Whalen. Senior Associate: Bryan Hale. Associates: Bina Bhattacharyya, Paul Zembsch. Team: Armando Amaral, Joshua Barkan, Philip Chan, Adrian Coleman, Johnny Cruz, Nikki Hartle, Jonathan Palmer-Hoffman, Amneris Rasuk, Tad Roemer, Kley Salas, Raymond Sih, Hilary Tate, Michael Weber. Associate Architect: HDR Architecture, Inc.

Robert A.M. Stern: Buildings and Projects 2004–2009 (New York: The Monacelli Press, 2009), 572–73.

Robert A.M. Stern: On Campus (New York: The Monacelli Press, 2010), 218–21.

Margot Carmichael Lester and Claire Parker, "Boulder, Colo.," *Architect*, March 2012.

"LEED Platinum for University of Colorado's New Biotechnology Building," *World Architecture News*, December 19, 2012.

House on Hook Pond
East Hampton, New York

Partner: Randy M. Correll. Project Manager: Timothy S. Deal. Team: Alexis M. Ryder.

Robert A.M. Stern: Buildings and Projects 2004–2009 (New York: The Monacelli Press, 2009), 597.

Designs for Living: Houses by Robert A.M. Stern Architects (New York: The Monacelli Press, 2014), 178–95.

Lana Bortolot, "Liquid Assets: From Hamptons Homes to Manhattan Townhouses, Robert A.M. Stern's Luxe Retreats Are Classic—With an Edge," *New York Post*, May 1, 2014, 33.

Bortolot, "Fab Five: For NYC's Tower Titans, Even the Most Rustic Homes Receive a Dramatic Touch of Grandeur," *New York Post*, May 1, 2014, 34.

Residential Colleges 13 and 14
Yale University, New Haven, Connecticut

Partners: Melissa DelVecchio, Graham S. Wyatt. Senior Associates: George de Brigard, Kurt Glauber, Christopher Heim, Sung Chan Park, Sara Rubenstein, Jennifer L. Stone, Marek Turzynski. Associates: Jennifer Bailey, Enid DeGracia, Ken Frank, Anya Grant, Kevin Hasselwander, Clay Hayles, Lara Kailian, Jonathan Kelly, Jennifer Lee, Tanya Lee, Christopher McIntire, George Punnoose, Kathleen Casanta Rasmussen, David Rinehart, Janice Rivera-Hall, Benjamin Salling, Colin Slaten, Mike Soriano, Leo Stevens, William West, Charles Yoo. Team: Rebecca Atkin, Alexander Boardman, Richard Box, Yolanda Cheung, Delia Conache, C. Gavet Douangvichit, Lindsay DuBosar, Elizabeth Baldwin Gray, Milton Hernandez, Alan Infante, Mia Gorgetti Layco, Kathryn Lenehan, Katherine LoBalbo, Marissa Looby, Matthew Masters, Asdren Matoshi, Anthony McConnell, Michael Mesko, Paul Naprestek, Cristian Oncescu, Therese Roche, Alex Rothe, Christopher Rountos, Michael Ryan, Christopher Rountos, Young Jin Yoon. Interior Design Associates: John Boyland, Lawrence Chabra, Philip Chan, Shannon Ratcliff. Interior Design Assistants: Megan Dohmlo, Crystal Palleschi. Landscape Design Senior Associate: Michael Weber. Model Builders: David Abecassis, Seth Burney, Victor Marcelino, Tehniyet Masood. Landscape Architect: OLIN.

Robert A.M. Stern: Buildings and Projects 2004–2009 (New York: The Monacelli Press, 2009), 578–79.

C.J. Hughes, "Yalies vs. Yale," *Architectural Record*, November 2009, 40.

"Updated College Renderings Released," *Yale Daily News*, September 9, 2010, 3.

Vivian Yee, "New College May Have Bells: Tower to Stand 26 Feet Shorter Than Harkness; Projected Opening Set for Fall 2015," *Yale Daily News*, September 24, 2010, 1, 6.

Egidio DiBenedetto, "Colleges Plan Submitted to City," *Yale Daily News*, October 1, 2010, 1, 6.

Alon Harish, "New Colleges Clear Hurdle," *Yale Daily News*, October 21, 2010, 1, 6.

David Brussat, "Beauty and Yale at New Haven," *The Providence Journal*, November 25, 2010.

"Yale's Thirteenth and Fourteenth Colleges," *Eli*, December 2010, 24.

Robert A.M. Stern: On Campus (New York: The Monacelli Press, 2010), 286–94, 304–9.

Thomas MacMillan, "$600M Project Wins Final Public Approval," *New Haven Independent*, January 4, 2011.

Carol Bass, "Approval, but No Start Date, for New Colleges," *Yale Alumni Magazine*, January 5, 2011.

Danny Serna, "New Colleges Approved," *Yale Daily News*, January 10, 2011, 3.

Kathrin Day Lassila, "Yale College: Still Expanding?" *Yale Alumni Magazine*, July/August 2011.

"Edward P. Bass Gift Puts Campaign Over Goal," *Eli*, September 2011, 2–5.

Nick Defiesta, "New Colleges Clear Final Hurdle," *Yale Daily News*, November 18, 2011.

Sophie Gould and Antonia Woodford, "New Colleges Filled With Singles," *Yale Daily News*, January 27, 2012.

Natasha Thondavadi, "With Mock-Up, Design Details of New Res Colleges Edited," *Yale Daily News*, February 24, 2012.

Tapley Stephenson and Natasha Thondavadi, "With Designs Set, New Colleges Waiting on Funding," *Yale Daily News*, April 6, 2012.

Natasha Thondavadi, "Firm Completes Renderings of Two New Colleges," *Yale Daily News*, April 10, 2012.

Tapley Stephenson, "Big Gifts on Horizon for Colleges," *Yale Daily News*, September 5, 2012.

Yanan Wang and Julia Zorthian, "Timeline for New Colleges Still Unclear," *Yale Daily News*, October 29, 2012, 1, 4.

Brendan Bashin-Sullivan, "The Giant Hole on Sachem Street," *Yale Daily News*, April 7, 2013.

Sophie Gould, "Construction on Campus Still Stalled," *Yale Daily News*, April 10, 2013, 1, 4.

Julia Zorthian, "Rumors Fly About New Colleges," *Yale Daily News*, September 27, 2013.

William Alden, "Mutual Fund Billionaire Gives $250 Million to Yale," *The New York Times*, September 30, 2013.

Matthew Lloyd-Thomas and Samuel Aber, "$250 Million Gift Propels Growth of New Colleges," *Yale Daily News*, October 1, 2013.

"The Largest Gift in Yale's History: Charles B. Johnson '54 Commits $250 Million to New Residential Colleges," *Eli*, Fall 2010, 6–9.

Adrian Rodrigues, "Colleges to Open in 2017," *Yale Daily News*, October 8, 2013.

Peter Salovey, "Our Educational Mission," *Yale Daily News*, October 14, 2013, 3.

Lucia Herrmann, "Neo-Gothic: Seriously?" *Yale Daily News*, November 21, 2013, 2.

Aaron M. Helfand, "Traditional Collegiate Architecture in America: A Timely Reassessment," *The Classicist*, No. 10, 6–27.

"A Mission to Expand Yale College: Donors Rally to Fund New College Construction," *Eli*, Winter 2014, 2–3.

Katy Osborn, "Robert and Robert," *The Yale Herald*, March 28, 2014.

Matthew Lloyd-Thomas and Adrian Rodrigues, "New Colleges Redesigned: New Colleges Will Have Doubles, More Students," *Yale Daily News*, April 11, 2014, 1, 4.

"Momentum Toward an Expanded Yale College," *Eli*, Summer 2014, 2–3.

Stayer Center for Executive Education
Mendoza College of Business, University of Notre Dame, Notre Dame, Indiana

Partners: Melissa DelVecchio, Preston J. Gumberich, Graham S. Wyatt. Associates: Christopher Heim, Kaveri Singh. Team: Richard Box, Timothy Carroll, Andreea Cojocaru, Melanie Fox, Daniel Hogan, Alan Infante, Mia Layco, Kathryn Lenehan, Erin Murphy, George Punnoose, Gregory Rachkovsky, David Revak, Michael Ryan, Mike Soriano, Jennifer L. Stone, Marek Turzynski. Interior Design Assistant: Megan Dohmlo. Model Builders: David Abecassis, Seth Burney, Victor Marcelion. Landscape Architect: Arkos Design.

Margaret Fosmoe, "Open for Business: ND's Executive Education Moves to New Building," *South Bend Tribune,* April 11, 2013, C:1.
Carol Elliott, "Notre Dame Executive MBA Jumps to No. 15 in *Bloomberg Businessweek* Ranking," *Notre Dame Today,* November 18, 2013.
"ND's Stayer Center—Made out of Gingerbread!" *Jim Small's ND Go Irish Blog,* December 18, 2013.

Product Design

DAVID EDWARD

Partner: Alexander P. Lamis. Senior Associate: Jeffery Povero. Project Manager: Nathaniel Pearson.

Robert A.M. Stern: Buildings and Projects 2004–2009 (New York: The Monacelli Press, 2009), 338–39.

BENTLEY PRINCE STREET

Partners: Alexander P. Lamis, Daniel Lobitz. Associates: Gaylin M. Bowie, John Boyland, Kyung Sook Gemma Kim. Project Managers: Kerim Eken, Nathaniel Pearson. Team: Motomi Morii.

Robert A.M. Stern: Buildings and Projects 2004–2009 (New York: The Monacelli Press, 2009), 338–39.
Kemp Harr, "Bentley Prince Street's Minite Discusses His Success With Design Collaboration," *Floor Focus,* July 2010, 21–22.
"Greening the School Office," *Architectural Products,* October 2012, 86.
"Bentley and CF Stinson," *Interior Design,* Show Daily 2014, 72.
"Bentley and CF Stinson: Light Play," *Contract,* June 2014, 64.
"Light Play," *Architectural Record,* July 2014, 53.

HADDONSTONE

Partner: Alexander P. Lamis. Senior Associate: Michael Weber. Project Manager: Nathaniel Pearson. Team: Alvaro Jose Soto.

Robert A.M. Stern: Buildings and Projects 2004–2009 (New York: The Monacelli Press, 2009), 338–39.

LANDSCAPE FORMS

Partner: Alexander P. Lamis. Senior Associate: Michael Weber. Project Manager: Nathaniel Pearson.

"Concord Site Furnishings," *Architectural Record,* January 2011, 126.

SA BAXTER

Partners: Alexander P. Lamis, Daniel Lobitz. Associates: Gaylin M. Bowie, Kyung Sook Gemma Kim. Project Managers: Kerim Eken, Nathaniel Pearson. Team: Motomi Morii.

"Door Man: It's Robert A.M. Stern at SA Baxter," *Interior Design,* January 2010, 38.
"Greek Theater," *Array,* June/July/August/September 2010, 45.
Mieke ten Have, "Turning Points," *Elle Décor,* September 2011, 236.
"The Classics," *Connecticut Cottages & Gardens,* March 2014, 36.

LUALDI

Partner: Alexander P. Lamis. Project Manager: Nathaniel Pearson.

Sharon McHugh, "Lualdi Opens Its Doors to American Designers," *World Architecture News,* October 25, 2010.
Tim McKeough, "More Than Just a Walk-Through," *The New York Times,* October 28, 2010, D:3.
"A New Door Opens," *Interior Design,* October 2010, 82.
"The Door That Says More," *Details,* December 2010.
"Grand Entrance," *Architectural Digest,* January 2011, 38.
"Lualdi American Designer Collection," *Architectural Record,* January 2011, 45.
"What's My Line: Test Your CT Design IQ," *Connecticut Cottages & Gardens,* September 2011, 40.
"Opening Statements," *Elle Décor,* November 2011, 100.

STINSON

Partners: Alexander P. Lamis, Daniel Lobitz. Associates: Gaylin M. Bowie, John Boyland, Kyung Sook Gemma Kim. Project Managers: Kerim Eken, Nathaniel Pearson. Team: Motomi Morii.

"World Tour," *Interior Design,* May 2011, 120.
"Products," *Hospitality Design,* March 2012, 85.
"Best of NeoCon 2012," *Contract,* July/August 2012, 70.
"Loud and Proud: Patterned Upholstery Steals the Show," *Interior Design,* August 2012, 118.
"Bentley and CF Stinson," *Interior Design,* Show Daily 2014, 72.
"Bentley and CF Stinson: Light Play," *Contract,* June 2014, 64.
"Light Play," *Architectural Record,* July 2014, 53.

WALKER ZANGER

Partners: Alexander P. Lamis, Daniel Lobitz. Associates: Gaylin M. Bowie, Kyung Sook Gemma Kim. Project Managers: Kerim Eken. Team: Motomi Morii.

Mayer Rus, "Elements of Style," *Architectural Digest,* September 2014, 36.

KINDEL / NEW YORK HOME COLLECTION

Partners: Alexander P. Lamis, Daniel Lobitz. Associates: Gaylin M. Bowie, John Boyland, Kyung Sook Gemma Kim. Project Managers: Kerim Eken, Sean Matijevich, Nathaniel Pearson. Team: Motomi Morii.

Anne Monoky, "*AD* Editors' Top Picks from the *Architectural Digest,* Home Design Show," *Architectural Digest,* April 3, 2012.
"Discoveries," *Architectural Digest,* July 2012, 28.
"Robert A.M. Stern's Sensibility Now in Furniture," *Robb Report,* July 31, 2012.
"What's Hot: Standing Ovation," *Elle Décor,* July / August 2012, 42.
"Comfort Scale," *Array,* June/July/August/September 2014, 53.

REMAINS

Partners: Alexander P. Lamis, Daniel Lobitz. Associates: Gaylin M. Bowie, Gemma Kim. Project Managers: Kerim Eken. Team: Motomi Morii.

Fitness and Aquatics Center
Brown University, Providence, Rhode Island

Partner: Gary L. Brewer. Project Managers: Christian N. Dickson, Eric Silinsh. Team: Matthew Blumenthal, Roland Flores, Kevin Hasselwander, Scott Hirshson, Miyun Kang, Justin Latham, Julie Nymann, Tad Roemer, Yoko Suzuki, Tin Lo, Tyler Vigil, Michael Weber, William Work. Interior Design Assistant: Crystal Palleschi. Landscape Architect: Rader Crews Landscape Architecture, LLP.

Robert A.M. Stern: Buildings and Projects 2004–2009 (New York: The Monacelli Press, 2009), 590.

Robert A.M. Stern: On Campus (New York: The Monacelli Press, 2010), 320–23.

Talia Kagan, "Fitness, Aquatics Center to Open in Jan. 2012," *The Brown Daily Herald,* March 16, 2010.

David Brussat, "Brown Sports to Sport Sporting New Digs," *The Providence Journal,* April 4, 2010.

David Brussat, "Brown's Unorthodox New Fitness Center," *The Providence Journal,* April 8, 2010.

David Brussat, "Bob Stern's Complex Contradictions," *The Providence Journal,* June 24, 2010.

David Brussat, "Update on Brown's Classical Nelson Fitness Center," *The Providence Journal,* September 22, 2011.

David Brussat, "Latest on Brewer's Fitness Center at Brown," *The Providence Journal,* November 19, 2011.

David Brussat, "Roses and Raspberries for 2011," *The Providence Journal,* January 5, 2012.

Richard Lewis, "Aquatics Center: Brown Dives Into Solar Energy," *Brown University News,* February 10, 2012.

Laura McLellan, "Solar-Thermal Panel Installation Largest in Country," *The Brown Daily Herald,* April 16, 2012.

David Brussat, "A Fine New Fitness Center at Brown," *The Providence Journal,* April 25, 2012.

Jasmine Bala, "New Fitness Center Overcomes Challenges," *The Brown Daily Herald,* November 14, 2012.

David Brussat, "Roses and Raspberries for 2012," *The Providence Journal,* January 17, 2013.

"Jonathan M. Nelson Fitness and Katherine Moran Coleman Aquatics Center, Brown University," *Athletic Business,* June 2013, 74.

William Morgan, "Brown: In Dissonance There's Harmony," *The Boston Globe,* December 3, 2013.

David Brussat, "An Elegant Guide to Brown's Campus," *The Providence Journal,* March 6, 2014.

"Fitness and Aquatics Center, Brown University," *The Classicist,* No. 11 (2014), 73.

Kohler Environmental Center
Choate Rosemary Hall, Wallingford, Connecticut

Partners: Kevin M. Smith, Graham S. Wyatt. Senior Associate: Jonas Goldberg. Project Manager: Brendan M. Lee. Team: Silas Jeffrey, Nasung Kim, Connie Osborn, Dennis Sagiev, Sue Jin Sung. Interior Design Associate: Shannon Ratcliff. Interior Design Assistants: Megan Dohmlo, Lisa Koch. Landscape Architect: Andropogon Associates, Ltd.

Jim H. Smith, "Living Green," *Bulletin: Choate Rosemary Hall Alumni Magazine,* Fall 2010, 8–14.

Luther Turmelle, "Work to Start Monday on $20 Million Choate Environmental Campus in Wallingford," *New Haven Register,* April 2, 2011.

Grace Merritt, "Choate to Build $20-Million Environmental Center," *The Hartford Courant,* March 31, 2011.

Dana Chivvis, "Graham Wyatt on Rethinking Schoolhouse Design," *NBC News Education Nation,* June 30, 2011.

Linda Tischler, "Prep Schools Lead the Way on Sustainable Living," *Fast Company,* October 3, 2011.

Howard R. Ernst, "Imagining a Green Future," *Bulletin: Choate Rosemary Hall Alumni Magazine,* Fall 2011, 64.

Luther Turmelle, "Choate Rosemary Hall's Kohler Environmental Center a Unique Space," *New Haven Register,* October 12, 2012.

James S. Russell, "Romney, Obama Avoid Climate Change Stigma, Waste Air," *Bloomberg,* October 25, 2012.

"Preppie Green," *The Hartford Courant,* November 19, 2012.

Wendy Carlson, "The Kohler Environmental Center: A Microcosm for Living and Learning," *Bulletin: Choate Rosemary Hall Alumni Magazine,* Fall 2012, 16–23.

"Live and Learn," *World Architecture News,* December 19, 2012.

James S. Russell, "Choate's Kids Wear Sweaters, Go Green, Eat Happy Chickens," *Bloomberg,* March 18, 2013.

Sebastian Jordana, "World Architecture Festival 2013: The Shortlist Has Arrived," *Huffington Post,* July 4, 2013.

Heart of Lake
Xiamen, China

Partners: Sargent C. Gardiner, Michael D. Jones, Grant F. Marani, Paul L. Whalen. Senior Associate: Rosa Maria Colina. Associates: Bina Bhattacharyya, Johnny Cruz, Nikki Hartle, Carlos Hurtado. Team: Joshua Barkan, Henry Chan, Thomas DiNatale, Lily Dong, Ian Greenberg, Juan Sebastian Munoz, Esther Park, Kley Salas, Megan St. Denis, Kenan Wei. Interior Design Associate: John Boyland. Interior Design Assistants: Tina Hu, Hyung Kee Lee, Alexandra Rolland. Associate Architect: BIAD. Interior Designer: RAMSI, Wilson Associates. Landscape Architects: OLIN, J&D Studio.

Alexei Barrionuevo, "When It Works in New York, They Take It on the Road," *The New York Times,* October 28, 2012, Real Estate: 1, 6.

Martin C. Pedersen, "The Charms of Suburbia," *Metropolis,* February 2014, 49–55.

"An Elegant, Thoughtful Community Rises in China," *CNU 2014 Charter Awards,* 2014, 20, 25.

Gerri C. LeBow Hall
LeBow College of Business, Drexel University, Philadelphia, Pennsylvania

Partners: Kevin M. Smith, Graham S. Wyatt. Associate: Douglas Neri. Team: Alexander Boardman, Lis Cena, Delia Conache, Joshua Feldman, Jonas Goldberg, Alan Infante, Francesca Singer, Sue Jin Sung, Bruce Yao. Interior Design Associate: Philip Chan. Interior Design Assistant: Crystal Palleschi. Associate Architect: Voith & Mactavish Architects, LP. Landscape Architect: Lager Raabe Skafte Landscape Architects.

CNU 2014 Charter Awards Booklet, 2014, 20, 25.

Melissa Dribben, "Drexel Alumnus Offers a $45 Million Gift," *The Philadelphia Inquirer,* November 16, 2010, A:1, 19.

"Drexel University's New Gerri C. LeBow Hall Opens for Business," *Drexel Now,* October 2, 2013.

Inga Saffron, "Drexel's New Business School Building Takes Its Surroundings Into Account," *The Philadelphia Inquirer,* November 30, 2013.

Jon Hurdle, "Drexel Works With Amtrak and Other Agencies to Freshen Up Philadelphia," *The New York Times,* April 9, 2014, B:8.

Chestnut Square
Drexel University, Philadelphia, Pennsylvania

Partners: Kevin M. Smith, Graham S. Wyatt. Associate: Douglas Neri. Team: Zeke Balan, Alexander Boardman, Lis Cena, Volkan Doda, Petr Dostal, Alan Infante, Lara Kailian, Jonathan Kelly, Donny Kim, Justin Latham, Renaud Magnaval, Christopher McIntire, William Perez, Eric Silinsh, Sue Jin Sung, Charles Yoo, Jef Zaborski, Paul Zembsch. Associate Architect: Voith & Mactavish Architects. Interior Designer: Sixth River Architects. Landscape Architect: Pennoni Engineering.

Natalie Kostelni, "Drexel University Project Will Have Retail and Student Housing," *Philadelphia Business Journal,* February 3, 2012.

Susan Snyder, "Drexel Plans Housing and Retail Project on Chestnut Street," *The Philadelphia Inquirer,* February 4, 2012.

Inga Saffron, "Drexel's Big Plans," *The Philadelphia Inquirer,* September 7, 2012.

Amy S. Rosenberg, "Temple and Drexel Reach Out With Upscale Dorms," *The Philadelphia Inquirer,* February 22, 2013.

Inga Saffron, "Apartment Towers Growing Toward Phila.'s West," *The Philadelphia Inquirer,* June 22, 2013.

Inga Saffron, "Granite Countertops, Flat-Screen TVs, Fire Pits: The Surprising Story of How College Dorms Got Luxe," *The New Republic,* September 18, 2013.

Amy Bigley Works, "Evolving Student Housing," *Northeast Real Estate Business,* May 2014, 26–27.

Cedarwoods
Willimantic, Connecticut

Partner: Grant F. Marani. Senior Associate: Charles Toothill. Associate: Megan St Denis. Team: Mario Cruzate, Esther Park, Michael Ryan. Associate Architect: Crosskey Architects. Landscape Architect: Ferrero Hixon Associates.

Laura Kusisto, "Housing Gets Architect Lift," *The Wall Street Journal,* April 18, 2013, A:20.

Louisa Owen Sonstroem, "Cedarwoods Opens—Officially," (Willimantic), April 19, 2013, 1, 4.

L. William Seidman Center
Seidman College of Business, Grand Valley State University, Grand Rapids, Michigan

Partners: Preston J. Gumberich, Graham S. Wyatt. Associates: Sean Foley, Celeste Hall, George Punnoose, Benjamin Salling, Kaveri Singh. Team: Delia Conache, Andreea Cojocaru, Thomas Fryer, Kevin Hasselwander, Alan Infante, Lara Kalian, Brendan Lee, Connie Osborn, Mark Rodriguez, Francesca Singer, Michael Weber, Charles Yoo. Interior Design Associate: Philip Chan. Interior Design Assistant: Marissa Savarese. Model Builders: David Abecassis, Seth Burney, Tehniyet Masood. Associate Architect: Integrated Architecture.

Dave Murray, "GVSU Debuts Plans for $40 Million Business School in Downtown Grand Rapids," *The Grand Rapids Press,* October 6, 2010.

Nancy Crawley, "Should Grand Rapids' Downtown Be Built by Local Talent Rather Than Starchitects?" *The Grand Rapids Press,* October 17, 2010.

Erin Albanese, "GVSU Leaders, Rich DeVos Gather for Seidman College of Business Groundbreaking," *The Grand Rapids Press,* May 25, 2011.

Dottie Barnes, "Center Symbolizes Modern Workforce, Underscores Modern Learning Environment," *Grand Valley Magazine,* Summer 2013, 33–38.

Leah Twilley, "Money Does Grow on Trees," *Grand Valley Magazine,* Summer 2013, 39.

House on Georgica Pond
East Hampton, New York

Partner: Randy M. Correll. Project Manager: Lenore Passavanti. Team: Nicholas Azevedo, Hannah Cho, Sho Okajima, Allen Philip Rohinson, Hilary Tate. Interior Designer: David Kleinberg Design Associates. Landscape Architect: Edmund D. Hollander Landscape Architect Design P.C.

Designs for Living: Houses by Robert A.M. Stern Architects (New York: The Monacelli Press, 2014), 262–83.

Lana Bortolot, "Fab Five: For NYC's Tower Titans, Even the Most Rustic Homes Received a Dramatic Touch of Grandeur," *New York Post,* May 1, 2014, 34.

Judith Nasir, "House Proud," *New York Spaces,* July/August 2014, 22.

Residence on Nassim Road
Singapore

Partners: Grant F. Marani, Paul L. Whalen. Associates: Nicholoas Azevedo, Mario Cruzate, David Winterton. Team: Joshua Barkan, Ariane Bibas, Gerard Beekman, Anthony Furino, Purva Jain, Esther Park, Kleber Salas, Megan St Denis, Eddie Zepeda. Interior Design Associate: John Boyland. Model Builder: David Abecassis. Associate Architect: RTQ.

Farrell Hall
Wake Forest Schools of Business, Wake Forest University, Winston-Salem, North Carolina

Partners: Kevin M. Smith, Graham S. Wyatt. Senior Associate: Breen Mahony. Project Manager: Marek Turzynski. Team: Delia Conache, Veronica Franzese, Ji-Hye Ham, Milton Hernandez, Alan Infante, Christian Oncescu, Connie Osborn, Slobodan Randjelovic, Mahdi Sabbagh, Marissa Savarese, Bruce Yao. Interior Design Associate: Philip Chan. Interior Design Assistant: Janice Wong. Landscape Design Senior Associate: Michael Weber. Landscape Design Project Manager: Mark Rodriguez.

Melissa Korn, "A Hall for Wake Forest," *The Wall Street Journal,* October 8, 2010, A:26.

Richard Craver,"$10M Gift for Wake Forest," *Winston-Salem Journal,* October 9, 2010, A:1, 2.

Julie Huggins, "Inside the New Wake Forest," *Old Gold & Black,* November 2, 2012.

Francesca Di Meglio, "New Wake Forest B-School Building Has a Living Room Feel," *Bloomberg Businessweek,* October 2, 2013.

Meghan Evans, "Business Hub: WFU Celebrates Official Dedication of Farrell Hall," *Winston-Salem Journal,* November 2, 2013, A:1, 9.

Ozark Hall
University of Arkansas, Fayetteville, Arkansas

Partner: Gary L. Brewer. Associate: Eric Silinsh. Team: Matthew Blumenthal. Interior Design Associate: Lawrence Chabra. Interior Design Assistant: Crystal Palleschi. Landscape Design Senior Associate: Michael Weber. Landscape Design Associate: Kevin Hasselwander. Associate Architect: Wittenberg, Delony & Davidson Architects.

"Back to the Future: Updating Ozark Hall," *A+,* 2012, 4–5.

Christopher James Palafox, "Cram Sessions," *American Builders Quarterly,* April/May/June 2014, 32–36.

Residential Tower at Xinyi
Taipei, Taiwan

Partners: Michael D. Jones, Paul L. Whalen. Senior Associates: Hernan Chebar, Chen-Huan Liao. Associate: Carlos Hurtado. Team: Armando Amaral, Lily Dong. Associate Architect: LKP Design.

Sunny Chiang, "Robert A.M. Stern," *La Vie Magazine (Taipei),* September 2012, 174–77.

Alexei Barrionuevo, "When It Works in New York, They Take It on the Road," *The New York Times,* October 28, 2012, Real Estate: 1, 6.

Abington House on the High Line
New York, New York

Partners: Daniel Lobitz, Paul L. Whalen. Associates: Gaylin M. Bowie, Enid De Gracia, Mike Soriano. Team: Johnny Cruz, Kyung Sook Gemma Kim, Chris Lee, Aileen Park. Interior Design Associate: John Boyland. Interior Design Assistant: Tina Hu, Hyung Kee Lee, Alexandra Rolland. Associate Architect: Ismael Levya Architects. Interior Designer: Clodagh Design. Landscape Architect: Matthews Neilsen.

Glenn Collins, "Near the High Line, a Parking Lot With High Ambition," *The New York Times,* May 25, 2011, A:24.

Pete Davies, "What Might Be Next for the High Line's Lot at 30th Street," *Curbed,* June 6, 2011.

Sara Polsky, "Starchitectural Craziness: Robert A.M. Stern Will Design Related's High Line Tower," *Curbed,* April 18, 2012.

Matt Chaban, "More Starchitecture for Hudson Yards! Robert A.M. Stern Bringing His Throwback Magic to 30th and 10th," *The New York Observer,* April 18, 2012.

Guelda Voien, "Related Wants Stores, Restaurants for Base of Tower Near Hudson Yards," *The Real Deal,* August 6, 2013.

Justin Davidson, "Unfashionably Fashionable: Robert A.M. Stern's Buildings Seem Like They've Always Been There," *New York,* November 11, 2013, 61–62, 87.

James Gardner, "A Building With Broad Shoulders: Related and Robert A.M. Stern Take Modest Look to New Extreme at High Line Rental," *The Real Deal,* January 2014, 66.

Jeremiah Budin, "The Amenity-Filled Abington House Starts Leasing This Month," *Curbed,* March 3, 2014.

Erin Carlyle, "On New York's High Line, a New Building Nods at the Past and Opens a Neighborhood," *Forbes,* April 7, 2014.

Mark Maurer, "Stern's Abington House Breaks Ranks With Other Starchitects," *The Real Deal,* April 8, 2014.

Anthony Paletta, "New Towers: Hit or Miss," *The Wall Street Journal,* May 5, 2014, A:24.

Josh Barro, "Affordable Housing That's Very Costly," *The New York Times,* June 8, 2014, Business: 1, 8.

"Hana R. Alberts, "Tour Robert A.M. Stern's High Line Rentals at Abington House," *Curbed,* July 10, 2014.

"Robert A.M. Stern's Abington House," *Departures,* July/August 2014, 96.

Navy Yard Master Plan Update
Philadelphia, Pennsylvania

Partners: Meghan L. McDermott, Graham S. Wyatt. Associates: Fredric Berthelot, Trevor Laubenstein. Team: Ryan Bostic, Veronica Francese, Nasung Kim, Matthew Masters, Charles Yoo. Model Builder: Victor Marcelino. Landscape Architect: Michael Van Valkenburgh Associates.

Robert A.M. Stern: Buildings and Projects 1999–2003 (New York: The Monacelli Press, 2003), 548–49.

Kellie Patrick Gates, "On the Brink of Reaching a 10,000-Jobs Milestone, Navy Yard Will Soon Release an Updated Master Plan," *Plan Philly,* September 20, 2012.

Linda Loyd, "Philadelphia Will Present Updated Plan for Navy Yard," *The Philadelphia Inquirer,* February 1, 2013.

Linda Loyd, "Navy Yard's Next Phase: The 2004 Master Plan Is Reworked to Reflect Success to Date," *The Philadelphia Inquirer,* February 3, 2013.

Natalie Kostelni, "Philadelphia's New King of Real Estate: John Gattuso Transforming Skyline Like Mentor Rouse," *Philadelphia Business Journal,* February 14, 2014, 1, 4–5.

World Business Council for Sustainable Development, *A Solutions Landscape for Philadelphia* (The Urban Infrastructure Initiative, 2013).

5 Crescent Drive
The Navy Yard, Philadelphia, Pennsylvania

Partners: Meghan L. McDermott, Graham S. Wyatt. Associates: Frederic J. Berthelot, Paul Zembsch. Team: Alexander Boardman, Anya Grant, Ji-Hye Ham, Jonathan Kelly, Nasung Kim, Katherine LoBalbo, Asdren Matoshi, Anthony McConnell, Nalina Moses, Sungchan Park, Sue Jin Sung, Charles Yoo, Young Jin Yoon, Jeff Zaborski. Interior Design Assistant (Base Building): Meghan Dohmlo. Landscape Design Senior Associate: Michael Weber. Landscape Design Project Manager: Kevin Hasselwander. Model Builder: Victor Marcelino. Associate Architect: Kendall/Heaton Associates, Inc. Interior Designer (Tenant Fit-Out): Francis Cauffman.

Natalie Kostelni, "GlaxoSmithKline Moving Phila. Operations to Navy Yard," *Philadelphia Business Journal,* February 8, 2011.

"Stern to Design Glaxo's Navy Yard Office," *The Philadelphia Inquirer,* February 8, 2011.

Inga Saffron, "What Does GlaxoSmithKline's Move to Navy Yard Mean for Downtown?" *The Philadelphia Inquirer,* February 18, 2011.

Diane Mastrull, "Move to Philadelphia's Navy Yard Will Be a Culture Shock for GlaxoSmithKline Employees," *The Philadelphia Inquirer,* March 6, 2011.

Ann Moline, "The Perfect Storm? Simultaneous Undercapacity and Overcapacity Pose Challenges for Biopharma Firms," *Site Selection,* March 2011, 216, 220–23.

Natalie Kostelni, "Slide Show: GlaxoSmithKline's Navy Yard Building Taking Shape," *Philadelphia Business Journal,* August 24, 2012.

Natalie Kostelni, "Throwing Away the Old Ways: GlaxoSmithKline's New Navy Yard HQ Will Have No Offices," *Philadelphia Business Journal,* August 24–30, 2012, 1, 9.

Inga Saffron, "Workplace Squatters at Glaxo's New Navy Yard Building," *The Philadelphia Inquirer,* March 22, 2013.

Inga Saffron, "Glaxo's New Building Carries Big Implications," *The Philadelphia Inquirer,* April 5, 2013.

"First Look: GlaxoSmithKline's Double LEED Platinum Office," *Building Design + Construction,* April 8, 2013.

Deane Madsen, "Double LEED Platinum for GSK's New Headquarters," *Architect,* April 10, 2013.

Stephanie Baum, "Standing Desks Aren't the Only Eye-Catchers at GSK's New Philly Digs," *MedCity,* April 11, 2013.

Linda G. Miller, "Rx for a Sustainable, Collaborative Corporate Building," *e-Oculus,* April 18, 2013.

"Five Crescent Drive," *ArchDaily,* April 24, 2013.

Elise Vider, "Pennsylvania's Five Coolest Green Buildings," *Keystone Edge,* May 16, 2013.

James McLachlan, "GlaxoSmithKline in Philadelphia's Old Navy Yard," *On Office Magazine,* May 24, 2014.

Karrie Jacobs, "Chiat's Triumph: The Ad Man Had Some Visionary Ideas About Workplace Design—20 Years Too Early," *Metropolis,* June 2013.

Emma Haslett, "Jazzy Offices Aren't Just for Trendy Start-Ups," *Management Today,* June 20, 2013.

John Gendall, "Forget the Office Park: GlaxoSmithKline's New Philadelphia Headquarters Shrank the Company's Footprint While Increasing Its Performance," *EcoStructure,* Winter 2013, cover, 42–49.

"Fostering Transparency," *Architecture+Design,* May 2014, cover, 34–38, 40, 42.

"Establishing a Sense of Place," *Architecture+Design,* May 2014, 32–33.

Immanuel Chapel
Virginia Theological Seminary, Alexandria, Virginia

Partner: Grant F. Marani. Senior Associates: Rosa Maria Colina, Charles Toothill. Associates: Esther Park, David Pearson, Leticia Wouk-Almino. Team: James Brackenhoff, Kevin Kelly, Marc Leverant, Marissa Looby, Katie Casanta Rasmussen, Frank Stevens, Mark Talbot, Jessie Turnbull, Chriska Wong. Landscape Architect: Michael Vergason Landscape Architects, Ltd. Liturgical Consultant: Terry Byrd Eason Design.

"Architects Chosen to Redesign Fire-Destroyed Virginia Seminary Chapel," *Episcopal News Service,* May 24, 2011.

Christy Goodman, "Theological Seminary to Build New Chapel," *The Washington Post,* May 25, 2011.

"Robert A.M. Stern Architects Tapped for Virginia Chapel," *World Architecture News,* May 26, 2011.

"Trustees Approve Plans for New Virginia Seminary Chapel," *Episcopal News Service,* November 22, 2011.

The Very Rev. Ian Markham, "A Board Engaged: An Historic Meeting at VTS," *News from the Hill,* December 2011, cover, 1, 18.

The Rev. James Barney Hawkins IV, "Retrospect and Prospect," *News from the Hill*, February 2013, 22–23.

Jeremy Bates, "Bells for Virginia Theological Seminary, Alexandria," *The Ringing World*, October 11, 2013, 1021–13.

The Rev. James Barney Hawkins IV, "Reflections on the Groundbreaking and the Chapel Garden Dedication," *News from the Hill*, October 2013, 26–27.

Residences on Zero Island
Tianjin, China

Partners: Grant F. Marani, Paul L. Whalen. Senior Associate: Victoria Baran, Rosa Maria Colina. Associates: Kevin Kelly, Esther Park, David Pearson, Kathleen Casanta Rasmussen. Team: James Brackenhoff, Katie Gillis, Elizabeth Baldwin Gray, Purva Jain, Julia Roberts, Jose Rodriguez, Huaxia Song, Frank Stevens, Mark Talbot, Michael Weber, Kenan Wei, Erica Weis. Landscape Design Senior Associate: Michael Weber. Landscape Design Assistant: Alex Rothe. Model Builder: Seth Burney. Associate Architect: Legend Real Property Consultant. Landscape Architect: OLIN.

Museum of the American Revolution
Philadelphia, Pennsylvania

Partners: Alexander P. Lamis, Kevin M. Smith. Senior Associates: Christopher Heim, Salvador E. Peña-Figueroa, Sara Rubenstein, Dennis Sagiev, Chuck Toothill. Associates: Thomas A. Lewis, Christopher LaSala, James Pearson, Susan Ryder. Team: Alexander Boardman, Breta Bishop, Kwei Chen Chang, Everald Colas, Molly Egan, Marc Leverant, Naomi Ocko, Raphael Ogoe, Hayeon Shim, Addie Suchorab, Mark Talbot, Jessie Turnbull, Alexander Vilcu, Albert Yadao. Interior Design Associate: Philip Chan. Interior Design Assistants: Suin Jung, Roger Tien, Janice Wong. Model Builders: David Abecassis, Liam Pittman. Landscape Architect: OLIN. Exhibit Designer: MFM Design.

Robert A.M. Stern: Buildings and Projects 2004–2009 (New York: The Monacelli Press, 2009), 308–11.

Melissa Dribben, "New Revolution Museum Plan: Robert A.M. Stern Is Again the Choice to Design the Site, Now in Center City," *The Philadelphia Inquirer*, November 1, 2011, A:1, 11.

Jenna McKnight, "Stern Chosen to Design American Revolution Museum in Philly," *Architectural Record*, November 1, 2011.

Robin Pogrebin, "Architect Named for Revolution Museum," *The New York Times*, November 2, 2011, C:3.

Nathaniel Popkin, "Shaping A Revolutionary Space: The New Museum of the American Revolution Must Be Relevant to Past, Present, and Future," *The Philadelphia Inquirer*, November 25, 2011.

Stephan Salisbury, "Lenfest Issues $40 Million Challenge for American Revolution Museum," *The Philadelphia Inquirer*, June 11, 2012.

Nathaniel Popkin, "Looking for Revolutionary Architecture? You won't find it at the New Museum of the American Revolution," *Hidden City Philadelphia*, June 11, 2012.

Robin Pogrebin, "Design Shown for Museum of American Revolution," *The New York Times*, June 12, 2012, C:1, 5.

Inga Saffron, "Revolution Lite: Robert A.M. Stern's Design for the Museum of the American Revolution Gets the Front Door and Ground Floor Right, but Just Pastes On Colonial Details," *The Philadelphia Inquirer*, June 12, 2012, C:1, 4.

"Robert A.M. Stern's Conservative Museum of the American Revolution Design Snuffs the Revolutionary Spirit," *Blouin Artinfo*, June 15, 2012.

David Brussat, "Revolutionary Revolutionary Museum," *The Providence Journal*, July 12, 2012.

David B. Brownlee, "Let's Make It Revolutionary," *The Philadelphia Inquirer*, August 21, 2012.

Liz Spikol, "A Scathing Review of Robert A.M. Stern's Philly Museum," *Curbed*, August 22, 2012.

Clem Labine, "Stern Gets Slammed for His Urban Civility," *Traditional Building*, October 12, 2012.

Clem Labine, "The Taliban of Architecture," *Traditional Building*, November 2012, 82.

Nathaniel Popkin, "At the Foot of the Mountain," *Hidden City Philadelphia*, November 25, 2012.

Inga Saffron, "Stern Rebuke: City Tells Museum Architect to Try Again," *The Philadelphia Inquirer*, February 17, 2014.

"Robert A.M. Stern Sent Back to Drawing Board for Revolutionary War Museum in Philadelphia," *Building Design + Construction*, February 18, 2014.

David Brussat, "Ramp It Up, Bob! Ramp It Up!" *Architecture Here and There*, February 18, 2014.

Ashley Hahn, "Where a Brick Is More Than a Brick," *Plan Philly*, March 6, 2014.

Nathaniel Popkin, "Design Revolution Needed," *The Philadelphia Inquirer*, March 7, 2014.

Nathaniel Popkin, "A Declaration of Architectural Independence: No Reactionary Design for a Revolution Museum!" *Change.org*, March 11, 2014.

Bradley Maule, "The Revolution, Stuck With Stern," *Hidden City Philadelphia*, April 3, 2014.

Maria Panaritis, "Key Approval for Museum of the American Revolution," *The Philadelphia Inquirer*, April 3, 2014.

Henry Melcher, "On Second Try, Robert Stern's Proposal for Philly's American Revolution Museum Approved," *The Architect's Newspaper*, April 7, 2014.

Liz Spikol, "A Stern Rejection: Philadelphia Seems to Be Stuck With the Robert De Niro of Architecture, and We Deserve Better," *Philadelphia*, May 2014, 134.

"Goodbye 1970s, Hello 18th Century at Third and Chestnut," *Philly Living*, May 6, 2014.

"Editorial: A Victory for Robert A.M. Stern Revolutionary War Museum," *The Philadelphia Inquirer*, June 10, 2014.

Damrak 70
Amsterdam, The Netherlands

Partners: Daniel Lobitz, Paul L. Whalen. Senior Associate: Hernan Chebar. Associate: Armando Amaral. Team: Kwei Cheng Chang, Dimitra Gelagoti, Chris Lee, Janice Rivera-Hall, Colin Slaten. Associate Architect: Rijnboutt Architects.

Tim Verlaan, "A Brutal(ist) Assault on Amsterdam's Inner City?" *Failed Architecture*, June 21, 2013.

Dalian AVIC International Square
Dalian, China

Partners: Michael D. Jones, Grant F. Marani, Paul L. Whalen. Senior Associate: Hernan Chebar. Associates: Armando Amaral, Bruce Yao. Project Manager: Janice Rivera-Hall. Team: James Brackenhoff, Kwei Cheng Chang, Rachael Fung, Dimitra Gelagoti, Georgina Harvey, Tanya Lee, Jennifer Lee, Ellee Lee, Elaine Lu, Nashin Mahtani, Monique Marian, Leo Mulvehill, Gali Osterwiel, Brad Shale, Mark Talbot, Jessie Turnbull, Chriska Wong, Way Wong, Kenan Wei. Associate Architect: Dalian Architecture Design Institute Co. Ltd. Landscape Architect: OLIN.

Alyssa Abkowitz, "A Chinese City's Parisian Love Affair," *The Wall Street Journal*, March 14, 2014, M:1, 8–9.

Barkli Residence
Moscow, Russia

Partners: Kevin M. Smith. Senior Associate: Dennis Sagiev. Associates: Douglas Neri, Benjamin Salling. Team: Zeke Balan, Lis Cena, William Gridley, Ji-Hye Ham, Brendan Hart, Renaud Magnaval, Asdren Matoshi, Benjamin Wescoe, Jef Zaborski. Associate Architect: Barkli Engineering.

Vladimir Belogolovsky, "Let's Not Play With History, Let's Do History: Interview With Robert A.M. Stern," *Tatlín News*, 2012, 62–67.

Egor Antoshenkov, "Architect Robert Stern: No Matter How Terrible Stalin Was, He Had a Wonderful Sense of the City," *PБK Daily*, November 15, 2013.

Olga Voronova, "Today the Sky Is the Limit," *Kommersant*, February 2014, Home and Interior: 11.

Schwarzman College
Tsinghua University, Beijing, China

Partners: Melissa DelVecchio, Graham S. Wyatt. Senior Associates: George de Brigard, Jonas Goldberg, Sung Chan Park. Associates: Jonathan Kelly, Paul Zembsch. Team: Delia Conache, Petr Dostal, Milton Hernandez, Ji-Hye Ham, Anthony McConnell, Paul Naprstek, Therese Roche, Jef Zaborski. Interior Design Partner: Alexander P. Lamis. Interior Design Associates: Lawrence Chabra, Philip Chan. Interior Design Assistant: Roger Tien. Associate Architect: AECOM.

Keith Bradsher, "$300 Million Scholarship for Study in China Signals a New Focus," *The New York Times*, April 21, 2013, 8.

Julia La Roche, "Billionaire Steve Schwarzman Has Donated $100 Million to Start His Own Version of the Rhodes Scholarship," *Business Insider*, April 21, 2013.

Andrew Browne and Lingling Wei, "Schwarzman Backs China Scholarship," *The Wall Street Journal*, April 22, 2013, C:3.

"College Breaks Ground in China to House $300 Million Scholarship Program by Blackstone Founder," *Associated Press*, October 24, 2013.

William C. Kirby, "The Chinese Century? The Challenges of Higher Education," *Daedalus, the Journal of the American Academy of Arts and Sciences*, Spring 2014, 145–56.

Hangyue Liangjiang Town Center
Chongqing, China

Partners: Michael D. Jones, Grant F. Marani, Paul L. Whalen. Senior Associates: Bina Bhattacharyya, Chen-Huan Liao. Associates: Kevin Kelly, Winnie Yen. Team: Jennifer Choe, Carlos Gamez, Katie Gillis, Stephanie Jazmines, Sam King, Anastasia Papadi, Julia Roberts, Jose Rodriguez, Huaxia Song, Foteinos Soulos, Matthew Standeven, Philippa Weston, Andrew Zelmer. Landscape Design Senior Associate: Michael Weber. Landscape Design Project Manager: Martha Desbiens. Landscape Design Assistants: Raa Boland, John Carluccio, Eric Drop, Di Hu, Rebecca Lederer, Svetlana Ragulina. Model Builder: Liam Pittman.

Heavener Hall
Heavener College of Business, Warrington College of Business Administration, University of Florida, Gainsville, Florida

Partners: Melissa DelVecchio, Graham S. Wyatt. Associates: Jennifer Bailey, Anya Grant. Team: Katherine LoBalbo, Matthew Masters. Interior Design Assistant: Kelsi Swank. Model Builder: Victor Marcelino. Associate Architect: Schenkel Shultz Architecture. Landscape Architect: David Connor and Associates, Inc.

"Project Briefs," *Florida/Caribbean Architect*, Summer 2013, 16–17.

Deluxe Bay
Jindong New District Master Plan, Jinhua, Zhejiang, China

Partners: Grant F. Marani, Paul L.Whalen. Associates: Nikki Hartle, Rosalind Tsang. Project Managers: Huaxia Song, Juenan Wu. Team: Johnny Cruz, Matt Lynch.

Northwestern Lake Forest Hospital
Lake Forest, Illinois

Partners: Augusta Barone, Kevin M. Smith, Graham S. Wyatt. Senior Associates: Jennifer L. Stone, Kim Yap. Associates: Christopher Heim. Team: Ryan Bostic, Jonathan Kelly, Anthony McConnell, Christian Oncescu. Landscape Design Senior Associate: Michael Weber. Landscape Design Assistant: Martha Desbiens. Model Builders: David Abecassis, Seth Burney, Luke Stricklin. Associate Architect: VOA Associates Inc.

1601 Vine Street
Philadelphia, Pennsylvania

Partners: Sargent C. Gardiner, Paul L. Whalen. Senior Associate: Bryan Hale. Associates: Johnny Cruz, Tanya Lee, David Rinehart, Janice Riviera-Hall, Benjamin Salling, Mike Soriano. Team: Marc DeSantis, Peter Garofalo, Caroline Grieco, Homin Jung, John Liu, Adam Lowenthal, Mason Meyer, Nicholas Mingrone, Liangie Otero, Johna Paolino, William Perez, Donny Silberman, Kyle Vreeland, JJ Yeo. Interior Design Senior Associate: John Boyland. Interior Design Associate: Philip Chan. Interior Design Assistants: Rowena Balan, Devin Borden. Landscape Design Senior Associate: Michael Weber. Landscape Design Project Manager: Stephen Koren. Landscape Design Assistants: Rana Boland, Eric Drop, Rebecca Lederer, Svetlana Ragulina, Eric Thomas. Model Builders: David Abecassis, Liam Pittman. Associate Architect: BLT Architects.

Natalie Kostelni, "New 32-Story Residential Tower Coming to Logan Square," *Philadelphia Business Journal*, February 12, 2014.

Laura McCrystal, "Mormons to Build 32-Story Tower in Center City," *The Philadelphia Inquirer*, February 12, 2014.

Jon Hurdle, "Mormon Church to Expand Development in Philadelphia," *The New York Times*, February 19, 2014, B:6.

Inga Saffron, "Mormon Development Combines Civic-Mindedness, Awful Architecture," *The Philadelphia Inquirer*, February 20, 2014.

New York Residences
AK Bulak, Astana, Kazakhstan

Partner: Grant F. Marani. Senior Associate: Rosa Maria Colina. Team: Michele Bruno, David Pearson, Frank Stevens. Assistants: Anastasia Krasnoslobodtseva, Amelia Kudenholdt, Ellee Lee.

ADDITIONAL PROJECTS

Apartment on Fifth Avenue
New York, New York

Partner: Roger H. Seifter. Associate: David Solomon. Interior Design: Michael Simon Interiors Inc.

Las Olas
Coral Isles, Fort Lauderdale, Florida

Partner: Roger H. Seifter. Associate: Joshua Bull. Team: Tiffany Barber, Josh Bartlett, Natalia Galvis, Megan St. Denis. Interior Design: Perlmutter-Freiwald. Landscape Architect: Rhett Roy.

Apartment at 15 Central Park West
New York, New York

Partner: Alexander P. Lamis, Roger H. Seifter. Project Manager: David Solomon. Interior Design Associate: John Boyland. Interior Design Assistants: Christina Berusch, Alexandra Rolland.

Harmony Cove
Trelawny, Jamaica, Project

Partner: Sargent C. Gardiner, Daniel Lobitz, Paul L. Whalen. Team: Monique Caron, Johnny Cruz, Lily Dong, Jonathan Pettibone, David Schellingerhoudt, Raymond Sih.

Brooklyn Law School Lobby
Brooklyn Law School, Brooklyn, New York

Partner: Paul L Whalen. Senior Associate: Hernan Chebar. Team: Kohilam Chandrahasan, Amneris Rasuk. Interior Design Assistant: Philip Chan.

Apartment at 820 Park Avenue
New York, New York

Partner: Roger H. Seifter. Associate: David Solomon. Team: Matthew Blumenthal, Laura Lisa DeLashmet, Brian Fell.

The Estates at Keswick Hall
Keswick, Virginia

Partners: Randy L. Correll, Daniel Lobitz, Grant F Marani, Roger H. Seifter. Associates: Gaylin M. Bowie, Brian Fell, Kyung Sook Gemma Kim. Team: Timothy S. Deal, Peter Garofalo, Chen-Huan Liao, Aileen Park, Hilary Tate. Model Builders: David Abecassis, Seth Burney, Tehniyet Masood.

Nick Kaye, "Breaking Ground: The Estates at Keswick Hall," *The New York Times*, February 5, 2010, C:32.
Larry Olmsted, "Second Homes, and Gardens, Grow in Charlottesville, Va.," *USA Today*, May 6, 2010.
Bob Morris, "Close to Campus: Enjoying the Many Pleasures of University Towns," *Robb Report Exceptional Properties*, January/February 2012, 50–52, 54, 56.

Mixed-Use Development
Boulogne-Billancourt, France, Competition

Partners: Meghan L. McDermott, Kevin M. Smith, Graham S. Wyatt. Associates: Fredric J. Berthelot, Don Lee. Project Manager: Renaud Magnaval. Team: Trevor Laubenstein, Asdren Matoshi, Jonathan Payne, Charles Yoo. Associate Architect: SRA Architectes. Landscape Architect: Mutabilis.

U.S. Courthouse
Billings, Montana, Competition

Partner: Grant F. Marani. Associate: Paul Zembsch. Team: Armando Amaral, Thomas DiNatale, Megan St. Denis. Associate Architect: HKS and Bitnar Architects. Landscape Architect: OLIN.

Redlich Hall
The Hotchkiss School, Lakeville, Connecticut

Partners: Preston J. Gumberich, Graham S. Wyatt. Associates: Sean Foley, Connie Osborn, George Punnoose. Team: Alexander Boardman, Delia Conache, Kenneth Fyfe, Alan Infante, Gregory Rachkovsky, David Rinehart, Mason Roberts, Therese Roche, Michael Ryan. Interior Design Associate: Philip Chan. Landscape Design Senior Associate: Michael Weber. Landscape Design Project Manager: Stephen Koren. Landscape Design Assistants: Rana Boland, Kevin Hasselwander. Model Builder: David Abecassis.

College of Law
University of Illinois at Urbana-Champaign, Urbana, Illinois, Project

Partners: Alexander P. Lamis, Daniel Lobitz. Senior Associate: Salvador Peña-Figueroa. Associates: Gaylin M. Bowie, Johnny Cruz, Kyung Sook Gemma Kim, Sara Rubenstein. Team: Deirdre Cerminaro, Aileen Park. Model Builders: Tehniyet Masood, Luke Stricklin. Associate Architect: Epstein. Landscape Architect: Jacobs/Ryan.

Colin Powell School for Civic and Global Leadership
CUNY/City College of New York, New York, New York, Competition

Partners: Augusta Barone, Graham S. Wyatt. Associate: Benjamin Salling. Team: Asdren Matoshi, Slobodan Randjelovic. Model Builder: David Abecassis.

Seorak Sorano
Hanwha Seorak Resort, Kangwondo, Korea

Partners: Kevin M. Smith, Graham S. Wyatt. Project Manager: Sue Jin Sung. Team: Benjamin Salling, Julia Huang, Nasuus Kim, Michael Ryan. Associate Architect: Gansam Partners.

Kim Tai Jip, *Gansam's Greatest Architecture* (Seoul: Artbook, 2013).

Apartment at 15 Central Park West
New York, New York

Partner: Roger H. Seifter. Senior Associate: Joshua Bull. Team: Tiffany Barber, Oscar Carlson, Laura Lisa DeLashmet, Ken Frank. Interior Design: John Gilmer Architect.

Capital City
Noida, Uttar Pradesh, India

Partners: Sargent C. Gardiner, Paul L. Whalen. Senior Associate: Bryan Hale. Associates: Johnny Cruz, Kley Salas. Team: Dominique Haggerty, Stephanie Jazmines, John Liu, Johna Paolino, Tad Roemer, Donny Silberman, Matthew Standeven, Donny Silberman, Kyle Vreeland, JJ Yeo. Associate Architect: RSP Design Consultants.

Matt Shoor, "India Seeks New York Firms for Exotic Designs," *e-Oculus*, April 6, 2011.
Dilasha Seth, "India Should Think Twice Before Rushing Skyward: Stern," *Business Standard*, September 13, 2012.

Becker Business Building
Barney Barnett School of Business, Florida Southern College

Partner: Alexander P. Lamis. Senior Associates: Salvador Peña-Figueroa, Sara Rubenstein. Associates: James Pearson, Susan Ryder. Team: Naomi Ocko, Addie Suchorab, Albert Yadao. Interior Design Associate: Philip Chan. Interior Design Assistant: Roger Tien. Landscape Design Senior Associate: Michael Weber. Landscape Design Assistants: Martha Desbiens, Svetlana Ragulina.

Shelley Rossetter, "Gift Will Help FSC Erect New Business Building," *The Ledger,* March 18, 2011.
"FSC to Name Building for Becker," *The Polk County Democrat,* March 26, 2011.
"FSC Receives Gift of New School: Donation Establishes Barney Barnett School of Business," *The Ledger,* April 28, 2011.
Mary Toothman, "Florida Southern to Begin Work on Site for Business College," *The Ledger,* February 14, 2013.

Residences on Mount Nicholson Road
Hong Kong

Partner: Grant F. Marani. Senior Associates: Rosa Maria Colina, David Winterton. Associates: Mario Cruzate, Megan St Denis. Team: Nicholas Acevedo, Louis Bond, Michele Bruno, Thomas DiNatale, Purva Jain, Brent Locey, David Pearson, Allen Robinson, Jose Rodriguez, Caroline Graf Statile, R. Craig Stevens, Frank Stevens, Mark Talbot, Erica Weiss, Way Wong, Eddie Zepeda. Interior Design Associate: John Boyland. Interior Design Assistant: Jamie Murphy, Alexandra Rolland. Landscape Design Senior Associate: Michael Weber. Landscape Design Project Managers: Martha Desbiens, Stephen Koren. Landscape Design Assistants: Rana Boland, John Carluccio. Associate Architects: Wong & Ouyang (HK) Ltd., Architects (AP) and LWK & Partners. Landscape Architect: OLIN.

House at West Chop
Vineyard Haven, Martha's Vineyard, Massachusetts

Partner: Gary L. Brewer. Associate: Winnie Yen. Team: Matthew Blumenthal. Landscape Design Senior Associate: Michael Weber. Landscape Design Associate: Kevin Hasselwander. Interior Designer: Kathryn Tate Interiors. Landscape Architect: Carly Look Design.

Student Residences on Lancaster Avenue
Villanova University, Villanova, Pennsylvania

Partners: Kevin M. Smith, Graham S. Wyatt. Senior Associate: Christopher Heim. Associates: Douglas Neri, Rosalind Tsang. Team: Zeke Balan, Caitlin Baransky, Alexander Boardman, Avnee Jetley, Rebecca Lischure, J. Javier Perez, Charlotte Smith. Associate Architect: Voith & Mactavish Architects, LP. Landscape Architect: Wells Appel.

Ashley Nguyen, "Dorm Projects a Staple of Main Line Campus Life," *The Philadelphia Inquirer,* October 6, 2011.
Ashley Nguyen, "Villanova's Plan to Expand Gets Off to Bumpy Public Start," *The Philadelphia Inquirer,* February 14, 2012.
Amy S. Rosenberg, "Temple and Drexel Reach Out With Upscale Dorms," *The Philadelphia Inquirer,* February 22, 2013.
Kathy Boccella, "Radnor Panel Rejects Villanova Expansion," *The Philadelphia Inquirer,* May 6, 2013.
Kathy Boccella, "Villanova Comes Back With New Expansion Plan," *The Philadelphia Inquirer,* September 23, 2013.
"Great Transformation," *Villanova Magazine,* Fall 2013, 19.
Linda Stein, "Radnor BOC Passed Villanova CICD Ordinance Allowing New Dorm, Performing Arts Center," *Mainline Media News,* April 1, 2014.
Natalie Kostelni, "Projects Finally Get Approved," *Philadelphia Business Journal,* April 18, 2014, 10.

Performance Arts Center
Villanova University, Villanova, Pennsylvania

Partners: Kevin M. Smith, Graham S. Wyatt. Senior Associate: Christopher Heim. Associates: Renaud Magnaval, Paul Zembsch. Team: Lis Cena, Ita Min Joo.

Residences on Barker Road
Hong Kong

Partner: Grant F. Marani. Senior Associate: Rosa Maria Colina. Associate: Mario Cruzate. Team: Michele Bruno, Michael Holt, Kevin Kelly, Esther Park, David Pearson, Megan St. Denis, Juenan Wu. Landscape Design Senior Associate: Michael Weber. Associate Architect: LWK & Partners Architects.

900 16th Street, NW
Washington, DC

Partner: Graham S. Wyatt. Senior Associates: Breen Mahoney, Marek Turzynski. Associates: Frederic J. Berthelot, Connie Osborn. Team: Delia Conache, Joshua Feldman, Veronica Franzese, William Gridley, Slobodan Randjelovic, Nina Voith. Interior Design Associates: John Boyland, Philip Chan. Associate Architect: Cooper Carry. Landscape Architect: Michael Vergason Landscape Architects, Ltd.

Jonathan O'Connell, "Robert A.M. Stern to Design 16th Street Church Project," *The Washington Post,* April 24, 2011.
Lydia DePillis, "New Third Church Almost Ready for Its Close-up," *Washington City Paper,* October 18, 2011.
Brady Holt, "After Demolition Skirmish, Church Unveils Latest Plans," *The Current,* October 19, 2011, 7, 19.
Lydia DePillis, "All-New 16th and Eye: Featuring Prism-tastic Third Church," *Washington City Paper,* November 4, 2011.
Anthony L. Harvey, "Proposed Design for 16th Street Complex to Replace Existing Brutalist Style Third Church Christ, Scientist, Near White House Well Received by Dupont Circle ANC," *The InTowner,* November 13, 2011.
David Alpert, "Preservationists Ask to Shrink 3rd Church Replacement," *Greater Greater Washington,* May 21, 2012.
Travis M. Andrews, "HPRB Votes Down 16th Street Mixed-Use Church and Office Building Design," *DC Mud,* May 25, 2012.
Jonathan O'Connell, "Brutalist Church Redevelopment Heads Back to Drawing Board," *The Washington Post,* May 29, 2012.
Elizabeth Wiener, "Historic Board Rejects Third Church Proposal," *The Northwest Current,* May 30, 2012.
Anthony J. Harvey, "HPRB Denies Height for 16th Street Office Building and Church Plan; Calls for Redesign," *The InTowner,* June 2012, 1, 5.
Daniel Sernovitz, "JBG Takes 68,000 Square Feet off the Table at 900 16th St. NW," *Washington Business Journal,* August 20, 2013.

Residences on Dun Hua South Road
Taipei, Taiwan

Partners: Sargent C. Gardiner, Grant F. Marani, Paul L. Whalen. Senior Associate: Bina Bhattacharyya. Associates: Johnny Cruz, Rosalind Tsang. Project Managers: Nikki Hartle. Team: Katie Gillis, Matt Lynch, Andrew Zelmer. Landscape Design Senior Associate: Michael Weber. Landscape Design Project Manager: Martha Desbiens. Landscape Design Assistant: Kevin Hasselwander. Model Builder: Seth Burney. Associate Architect: HOY Architects & Associates. Landscape Architect: Horizon & Atmosphere Landscape Co.

Residence
Mountain Lake, Florida

Partner: Roger H. Seifter. Senior Associates: Victoria Baran, Joshua Bull. Team: Sean Blackwell, Cristiana Pledger. Interior Design: Buzz Kelly. Landscape Design: Morgan Wheelock.

Residence in Golf Links
New Delhi, India

Partners: Roger H. Seifter, Paul L. Whalen. Senior Associates: Victoria Baran, Hernan Chebar. Associates: Gerard Beekman, Christian N. Dickson. Team: Tim Carroll, Hannah Cho, Nicholas DeRosa, Brent Locey, David Rinehart, Christopher Rountos, Caroline Graf Statile. Associate Architect: We Design.

Dilasha Seth, "India Should Think Twice Before Rushing Skyward: Stern," *Business Standard*, September 13, 2012.

31 Conduit Road
Hong Kong

Partners: Sargent C. Gardiner, Grant F. Marani, Paul L. Whalen. Senior Associate: Bina Bhattacharyya. Associates: Johnny Cruz, Kley Salas, Rosalind Tsang. Project Managers: Josh Barkan. Team: Katie Gillis, Andrew Zelmer. Interior Design Associate: Lawrence Chabra. Landscape Design Senior Associate: Michael Weber. Landscape Design Assistant: Martha Desbiens. Model Builder: Seth Burney. Associate Architect: P&T Architects & Engineers.

Sunny Chiang, "Interview With Robert A.M. Stern," *La Vie*, September 2012, 174–77.

Arris
1331 4th Street, SE, The Yards, Washington, DC

Partners: Sargent C. Gardiner, Paul L. Whalen. Associate: Peter Garofalo. Project Manager: Tanya Lee. Team: Loke Chan, Adam Lowenthal, Janice Rivera-Hall, Tad Roemer, Tim Slater. Interior Design Associate: John Boyland. Interior Design Assistants: Megan Dohmlo, Bennett Leifer, Cara Zelikovsky. Landscape Design Senior Associate: Michael Weber. Landscape Design Project Managers: Kevin Hasselwander, Stephen Koren. Landscape Design Project Assistant: Eric Drop. Associate Architect: WDG Architecture.

Amanda Wilson, "First Look at Parcel N at the Yards," *DC Mud*, December 28, 2012.
Michael Neibauer, "Up With Forest City's 327-Unit Arris and GW's Massive New Dorm," *Washington Business Journal*, August 18, 2014.

15 LEGO Park West
Model for the National Building Museum's Exhibit "LEGO Architecture: Towering Ambition"

Project Manager: Jonathan Grzywacz.

"New Architectural Models Added to LEGO® Architecture Exhibition," *National Building Museum*, April 2, 2012.
Alexander Maymind and Matthew Persinger, "Manhattanisms: RAM(s) vs. REM," *Pidgin*, Issue 11 (2012), 208–19.

Admissions Building
Elon University, Elon, North Carolina

Partners: Kevin M. Smith, Graham S. Wyatt. Project Manager: Silas Jeffrey. Team: Ryan Bostic, Petr Dostal, Ken Frank, Victor Marcelino, Marek Turzynski, Young Jin Yoon, Jef Zaborski. Interior Design Associate: Philip Chan. Model Builder: Victor Marcelino.

School of Communications
Elon University, Elon, North Carolina

Partners: Kevin M. Smith, Graham S. Wyatt. Senior Associate: Marek Turzynski. Project Manager: Silas Jeffrey. Team: Ryan Bostic, Petr Dostal, Kenneth Frank, Young Jin Yoon, Jef Zaborski. Interior Design Associate: Philip Chan. Model Builder: Victor Marcelino.

Michael Bodley, "Design for McEwen School of Communications Finalized, Plans Continue to Develop," *The Pendulum: Elon University's Student News Organization*, September 16, 2013.

House in Edgartown
Martha's Vineyard, Massachusetts

Partner: Gary L. Brewer. Associate: C. Callaway Hayles.

Gatton College of Business and Economics
University of Kentucky, Lexington, Kentucky

Partners: Kevin M. Smith, Graham S. Wyatt. Senior Associate: Christopher Heim. Associate: Douglas Neri. Team: Zeke Balan, Petr Dostal, William Gridley, Brendan Hart, Alan Infante, Jennifer Lee, David Rinehart, Benjamin Wescoe, Jef Zaborski. Interior Design Associate: Philip Chan. Associate Architect: Ross Tarrant Architects.

Linda Blackford, "Start of UK Gatton Building Expansion Helps Show Success of Private Funding Options," *Lexington Herald-Leader*, October 11, 2013.

Shepherd University Master Plan
Shepherdstown, West Virginia

Partners: Augusta Barone, Graham S. Wyatt. Senior Associate: Jennifer L. Stone. Team: Young Jin Yoon. Landscape Design Senior Associate: Michael Weber. Landscape Design Assistant: Svetlana Ragulina.

Jenni Vincent, "Shepherd Has New 10-Year Master Plan," *The Journal* (Martinsburg, West Virginia), May 19, 2013.

Correll Hall
Terry College of Business, University of Georgia, Athens, Georgia

Partners: Kevin M. Smith, Graham S. Wyatt. Senior Associates: Dennis Sagiev, Jennifer L. Stone. Associates: Ken Frank, Benjamin C. Salling. Team: Ryan Bostic. Interior Design Associate: Philip Chan. Interior Design Assistants: Suin Jung, Cara Zelikovsky. Associate Architect: Rule Joy Trammell + Rubio, LLC.

Lee Shearer, "Work Beginning on Three Big UGA Construction Projects," *Athens Banner-Herald*, February 1, 2013.
Erin Zlomek, "Funding for New Georgia B-School Almost Complete," *Bloomberg Businessweek*, May 7, 2013.
Blake Aued, "This New UGA Terry College Building Looks Like a Church," *Flagpole*, May 1, 2013.

Three Otter Farm
Edgartown, Martha's Vineyard, Massachusetts

Partner: Roger H. Seifter. Senior Associates: Victoria Baran, Brian Fell. Associates: Christopher McIntire, Caroline Graf Statile, Allen Robinson, C. Callaway Hayles. Team: Tiffany Barber, Craig Chowaniec, Katherine LoBalbo, Christian Mueller, Ryan Salvatore. Interior Design Assistants: Ann Baumgartner, Alexandra Roland, Cara Zelikovsky. Landscape Design Senior Associate: Michael Weber. Landscape Design Project Manager: Natalie Ross. Landscape Design Assistant: Rebecca Lederer, Svetlana Ragulina.

Pezet I
San Isidro, Lima, Peru

Partners: Michael D. Jones, Paul L. Whalen. Senior Associate: Rosa Maria Colina. Associates: Nicholas Acevedo, Kley Salas, Carlos Hurtado. Team: Johna Paolino, Natalie Pierro, Han Tuan, Phillipa Weston. Associate Architect: ACM Holding.

College of Business Administration
University of Nebraska, Lincoln, Nebraska

Partners: Melissa DelVecchio, Graham S. Wyatt. Associates: Frederic J. Berthelot, Anya Grant, Kaveri Singh, Colin Slaten, Paul Zembsch. Team: Alan Alexander, Caitlin Baransky, Andreea Cojocaru, C. Gavet Douangvichit, Asdren Matoshi, Stephanie Medel, Jesus Alejandro Guerrero Vera, Sheng Wu, Jef Zaborski. Interior Design Associate: Philip Chan. Interior Design Assistant: Suin Jung. Model Builder: Tehniyet Masood. Associate Architect: Alley Poyner Macchietto Architecture, P.C. Landscape Architect: Sasaki Associates, Inc.

"CBA Building Architects Chosen, Donors Recognized," *Lincoln Journal-Star*, March 21, 2013.
Leslie Reed, "Major Donations Fuel UNL's $84 Million Business College Project," *Omaha World-Herald*, March 22, 2013.
"UNL Progresses With Funds, Architects for New CBA Building," *Daily Nebraskan*, March 28, 2013.

Additions to the International Tennis Hall of Fame
Newport, Rhode Island

Partner: Gary L. Brewer. Associate: Katie Casanta Rasmussen, Eric Silinsh. Team: Sean Blackwell, Katherine Hanson, C. Callaway Hayles, Anastasia Krasnoslabodtseva, Christopher Lucas, Joseph Yatco. Interior Design Associate: Lawrence Chabra.

Sean Flynn, "Hall of Fame Project Clears First Hurdle," *The Newport Daily News*, December 10, 2013, A:1, 6.
Sean Flynn, "Tennis Hall of Fame Project Moves Forward," *The Newport Daily News*, January 29, 2014, A:1, 10.
Donita Naylor, "Ground Broken for $15.7 Million Expansion of Newport's International Tennis Hall of Fame," *Providence Journal*, May 14, 2014.

Blossom Plaza
Santa Monica, California, Competition

Partners: Sargent C. Gardiner, Paul L. Whalen. Senior Associate: Bryan Hale. Associate: Tanya Lee. Team: Ava Amirahmadi, John Liu, Adam Lowenthal, Johna Paolino, Timothy Slater, Kyle Vreeland, JJ Yeo. Model Builders: David Abecassis, Victor Marcelino, Tehniyet Masood.

Sam Lubell, "And They're Off: Santa Monica Selects Design/Development Teams for Major Downtown Project," *The Architect's Newspaper*, March 1, 2013.
Guy Horton, "Downtown Dutch: Santa Monica Chooses OMA for Major Mixed-Use Project," *The Architect's Newspaper (West)*, August 14, 2013, 1, 4.

Courier Square
Charleston, South Carolina

Partner: Gary L. Brewer. Associate: Eric Silinsh. Assistants: Matthew Blumenthal, Adeola Oshodi, Winnie Yen. Associate Architect: LS3P. Landscape Architect: DesignWorks, LLC.

Paul Bowers, "P&C Parent Company Planning Development at Meeting and Columbus," *Charleston City Paper*, May 24, 2013.
Schuyler Kropf, "Architectural Review Board Defers on Meeting St. Apartment and Retail Plans," *The Post and Courier*, December 3, 2013.
Corey Davis, "Massive Downtown Development 'Game Changer' If Approved," WCSC, December 3, 2013.
David Slade, "Courier Square Would Be Test Case for New Zoning With 100-Foot Height Limit," *The Post and Courier*, January 15, 2014.
Schuyler Kropf, "Courier Square Receives Early BAR Approval," *The Post and Courier*, February 26, 2014.

House at Jackstay Court
Kiawah Island, South Carolina

Partner: Gary L. Brewer. Associate: C. Callaway Hayles. Team: Fernanda Naveria-Castro, Mason Roberts. Landscape Architect: DesignWorks, LLC.

Hoover Dining Hall
DePauw University, Greencastle, Indiana

Partners: Preston J. Gumberich, Graham S. Wyatt. Associates: Sean Foley, George Punnoose, Connie Osborn. Team: Delia Conache, Alan Infante, Jonathan Kelly, Anthony McConnell, Daniel Ottochian, Mason Roberts, Marek Turzynski. Interior Design Associate: Philip Chan. Interior Design Assistant: Rachel Kim. Landscape Design Senior Associate: Michael Weber. Landscape Design Assistants: Eric Drop, Stephen Koren. Model Builder: David Abecassis.

Brock Turner, "Budget Concerns Growing Ahead of Hoover Dining Hall Construction," *The DePauw*, February 4, 2014.
"University Breaks Ground on Hoover Dining Hall," *DePauw*, May 17, 2014.

Angelo, Gordon & Co.
New York, New York

Partners: Randy M. Correll, Alexander P. Lamis. Senior Associate: Charles H. Toothill. Associates: Thomas Lewis, R. Craigh Stevens. Project Manager: Alexis M. Ryder. Team: Molly Egan, Caroline Grieco, Paul-Arthur Heller, Jessie Turnbull, Alex Wilson. Interior Design Associate: John Boyland. Interior Design Project Manager: Lauren Kruegel. Interior Design Assistants: Eda Alpaslan, Doug West.

Lake House
Lakeside, Michigan

Partner: Randy M. Correll. Associates: Timothy S. Deal, Allen Phillip Robinson. Team: Nicole Kotsis. Interior Designer: Arthur Dunnam of Jed Johnson Associates. Landscape Architect: Philip Rosborough of Rosborough Partners.

House on Eugenia Avenue
Kiawah Island, South Carolina

Partner: Gary L. Brewer. Associates: C. Callaway Hayles, Katie Casanta Rasmussen, Eric Silinsh. Team: Adeola Oshodi, Kenan Wei.

Illustration Credits

Photographers

Peter Aaron / OTTO: front cover, 13–17, 18 (middle), 32–36, 37 (top), 38–43, 53–63, 70–89, 102–109, 130–157, 159–162, 178–179, 181–189, 192–219, 226–235, 239–253, 274–284, 285 (bottom), 286–289, 302–319, 328 (bottom), 329–333, 336–353, 357–363, 424 (1), 425 (1), 426 (4), back cover

Aedas: 164–167

SA Baxter: 273 (right top, right middle)

David Edward: 273 (right bottom)

Francis Dzikowski: 18 (top, bottom), 19–25, 44–51, 64–69, 90–97, 110–123, 125–129, 168–173, 260–269, 320–327, 366–369, 424 (5)

Scott Frances: 424 (3)

Halkin Mason Photography: 370–373

Landscape Forms: 271 (right bottom)

Lualdi: 272 (left)

Alise O'Brien: 28–31

OxBlue: 374

Jock Pottle: 180, 270 (top), 271 (top, left bottom), 272 (right), 273 (left bottom),

Zak Powers: 124

Robert A.M. Stern Architects: 238, 273 (left top), 290–291, 294–295, 296 (bottom), 297, 299, 328 (top), 334–335, 354, 377, 396–397, 410, 412–413, 424 (2 right), 428 (4), 429 (3)

Stinson: 270 (bottom)

David Sundberg / Esto: 2, 99–101

Jeffrey Totaro: 27

Stefen Turner: 285 (top)

University of Colorado: 236

Vanke Real Estate Enterprise: 292–293, 296 (top), 298, 300–301

Les Vants Aerial Photos: 37 (bottom)

Peter Vitale: 190–191

Zeckendorf Development: 163

Renderers

ACM Grupo: 431 (1)

Aerial Photography Inc.: 424 (2 left)

Archpartners: 175–177

Art 3D: 401

AVIC International Holding Corporation: 388–393, 395

Chongqing Hangyue Real Estate Company: 408–409

Clover Architectural Rendering: 378, 418–421, 428 (1)

dbox: 255–259

Gil Gorski: 424 (4), 425 (3)

Jinhua Dongchen Real Estate Development: 412

Michael McCann: 425 (2 left), 431 (3, 5)

Jeff McSwain: 427 (3), 430 (1), 432 (1, 5)

MFM Design: 383

NC3D: 381, 429 (4, 5)

Neoscape: 364–365, 402–407, 431 (4)

Thomas Schaller: 427 (1)

The Seventh Art: 221, 223–225

Clark Smith: 425 (2 right), 428 (5)

Dick Sneary: 379

Robert A.M. Stern Architects: 222, 237, 254, 385 (top), 394, 417, 425 (5), 426 (2, 5), 428 (2, 3), 429 (1, 2), 430 (5), 432 (3, 4)

Jeff Stikeman: 284, 375–376, 410–411, 414–415, 426 (1, 3), 427 (4, 5), 431 (2), 432 (2)

studio amd: 399–400, 425 (3), 430 (2, 4)

Top Vastgoed Planontwikkeling BV: 385 (bottom), 386–387

Wheelock Properties Limited: 427 (2)

Win Sing Development: 355

Library of Congress Control Number
2014946563

ISBN 978-1-58093-402-2

Printed in Canada

10 9 8 7 6 5 4 3 2 1
First edition

Designed by Pentagram

www.monacellipress.com